SIMPLY EGGPLANT

Simply Eggplant

Kosher Recipes From Around the World

by

Shirley Smalheiser

gefen גפן
publishing house בית הוצאה לאור
JERUSALEM ♦ NEW YORK

Typesetting: Marzel A.S. – Jerusalem

Cover Design: Studio Paz, Jerusalem

Edition 9 8 7 6 5 4 3 2 1

Gefen Publishing House
POB 36004
Jerusalem 91360, Israel
972-2-538-0247
isragefe@netvision.net.il

Gefen Books
12 New Street
Hewlett, NY 11557, USA
516-295-2805
gefenbooks@compuserve.com

www.israelbooks.com

Printed in Israel   *Send for our free catalogue*

Library of Congress Cataloging-in-Publication Data
Smalheiser, Shirley.
Simply Eggplant: Kosher Recipes From Around the World / by Shirley Smalheiser

ISBN: 965 229 204 4

1. Cookery (Eggplant). 2. Cookery, International. I. Title.
TX803.E4S63 2000
641.6'5646—dc21
                                                                    99-40467
                                                                       CIP

Contents

Beef Recipes

Vegetable Recipes

Beans, Grains & Pasta

Desserts & Sweets

Miscellaneous Recipes

Preface

One evening, not too long ago, as my husband and I sat down to dinner, he remarked that I prepared eggplant so often, and in so many different ways, that he has come to expect eggplant to be served with almost every meal. But, he added, I prepared it so ingeniously that he often cannot identify the eggplant dish.

His comment made me realize a terrible truth about myself. I had become an "eggplant junkie". My earliest memories of food are of the fried eggplant my mother made. She fried slices in sweet butter until they were golden brown with a center as soft as custard. Sometimes, she would first dip the slices in a beaten egg and coat with seasoned cornflake crumbs. I still recall the delight I felt when biting into those crunchy morsels.

My passion for eggplant stayed with me after I grew up and I prepared my own meals. It seemed natural that eggplant should have an honored place on our table. As time went on and I traveled the United States and other countries around the world, I was amazed to find that this one simple vegetable can be made in hundreds of ways.

The secret seems to be the affinity that eggplant has for many different foods and seasonings. The Italians combine eggplant with onion, tomatoes, garlic and basil. Chinese cooks use garlic, ginger and soy sauce. An Indian dish will use garam masala, turmeric and cumin. In each, the eggplant is transformed so that it tastes differently from recipe to recipe, from country to country.

My eggplant recipe collection became the talk of the neighborhood, and I was often asked for suggestions about new ways to prepare my favorite vegetable. Finally, one day, observing how the collection had taken over most of a file cabinet, my husband made a fateful suggestion: "You ought to write an eggplant cookbook." And so I did.

In this book are my favorite eggplant recipes. Many are variations of classics, such as Greek Moussaka, Italian Eggplant Parmigiana and French Ratatouille. Others are ethnic foods, such as Hunan Style Eggplant from China, Eggplant Salad with Mayonnaise from Israel, Indonesian Beef and Green Beans, and North African Turkey Balls from Morocco.

I also created many tantilizing new dishes by incorporating eggplant into traditional recipes which ordinarily do not include eggplant: chili (Spicy Beefy Chili), beef stew (Italian Beef Stew), and meat loaf (Greek Meatloaf).

No longer need you rely on the same old eggplant dishes. Here you will find a wealth of recipes for eggplant salads, soups, main meals and even desserts I devised. Your guests will never guess that my Mock Pumpkin Mousse and Chocolate Eggplant Drop Cookies owe their tantilizing flavor to eggplant.

This book is subtitled *"A Kosher Cookbook"* because each recipe conforms to Jewish dietary laws. In very simplified terms, these laws prohibit eating dairy products with meat or poultry. In addition, certain foods are neutral ("parve") and may be eaten with either dairy products or meat and poultry.

Those households which keep a kosher kitchen understand the complexities of these dietary laws. However, the book is written for anyone who wants to enjoy the superb culinary range and taste of eggplant.

Be warned: with so many exciting recipes to try, you too may become an "eggplant junkie."

Shirley Smalheiser
Mitzpe Ramon, Israel
January, 2000

Everything You Ever Wanted To Know About Eggplant & More

Why a cookbook devoted to eggplant? Because western cooks are fast becoming aware of what European, Middle Eastern, North African and Asian cooks have known for centuries: that eggplant has unique characteristics among vegetables.

It has the capacity to absorb the flavors of the foods and spices with which it is cooked, and therefore, in different recipes it tastes differently. Equally important: eggplant enhances the flavors of other foods. These features enable it to combine well with most every other type of food to produce delicious meals.

Add to these characteristics the facts that eggplant is inexpensive, nutritious in itself and available year round and one can understand why eggplant has achieved the reputation of a wonder vegetable among its aficionados.

History and Folklore

Eggplant has been cultivated as a vegetable since remote antiquity. Agronomists believe that it originated in Asia, perhaps in India or China. Arab traders brought eggplant to the Middle East in the 7th century and the Moors introduced it to Spain with their conquest in the early 8th century.

Its use then spread to Portugal, southern France and southern Italy. Pope Pius IV (1559-1566) was so taken with eggplant that he greeted guests with welcoming gifts of the plant. Eventually, Spanish explorers carried eggplant to the New World in their conquest of the Caribbean and Mexico in the 16th century.

Eggplant developed into an integral part of the cuisines of the countries bordering on the Mediterranean: southern Europe (Italy, France, Greece), North Africa (Morocco, Algeria, Egypt), and the Middle East (Israel, Lebanon, Syria, Turkey). In addition, eggplant is still a key ingredient in the diets of many Asian nations where it originated (India, Thailand, China, Japan).

Apart from its function as food, eggplant is supposed to have medicinal qualities. In Nigeria, it is highly regarded as a treatment for convulsions and rheumatism. Traditional healers in Korea prescribe dried eggplant as a treatment for lumbago, measles, stomach cancer and alcoholism. The Chinese use eggplant as a teeth whitener, while grandmothers elsewhere recommend chewing a raw slice of eggplant as a cure for constipation.

Eggplant is also one of the many vegetables from which paper can be made. The Papyrus Institute of Cairo makes eggplant paper in 9x12 sheets which can be bought from Carriage House Paper, 79 Guernsey Street, Brooklyn, New York, 11222. For the hobbiest, Carriage House Paper also sells a booklet entitled Vegetable Papyrus, by Maureen Richardson which explains how to make papyrus from eggplant as well as other vegetables.

Eggplant has achieved an interesting status in literature. In *Love In The Time Of Cholera* by Nobel Prize winning author Gabriel Garcia Marquez (first English translation published by Alfred A. Knopf, Inc, New York 1988), the heroine's changing attitude toward eggplant, from violent dislike to passionate fondness, symbolizes her emotional growth.

Eggplant plays quite a different role in John Barth's *The Sot-Weed Factor* (Revised edition, Doubleday, 1987). That novel purports to tell the true story of how Captain John Smith won Pocahontas. Curious readers who would like to know how he ingeniously used eggplant to relieve her of her maidenhood are referred to the book.

By the way, while eggplant is the name most often used for this vegetable, in parts of Africa it is called eggfruit and guinea squash. And in France, to be different, it is known as aubergine. That too was the rather disparaging name the French applied to the meter maids who wore purple uniforms as they patrolled the streets, giving out parking tickets: they were called aubergines – until their uniform changed to blue. Now they are called pervenche, after the name of a blue flower.

It may have occured to you that eggplant is semantically unique among vegetables in that its name includes the word "plant" and the same word applies both to the plant and to its fruit. You plant seeds to grow eggplant (plants) and at the end of the growing season, you harvest eggplants.

Cultivation Today

Technically, eggplant (Solanum melongena) is a tender perennial plant of the nightshade family (solanaceae) that is usually grown as an annual. It is related to the tomato in that both grow above ground and have seeds, but it is nutritiously similar to the potato.

Eggplant needs a long warm weather growing season. Night-time temperature should not drop below 55 F for any extended period. Beginning in February or March, seedlings are grown in heated plastic or glass enclosures for about 8 weeks before transplanting. Strong healthy plants, 6 to 8 inches tall, are best for field setting.

Eggplants need space: they are transplanted at 2½ foot intervals, in rows three feet apart. A drip irrigation system is best to satisfy the eggplant's thirst for water. A single plant grows to a height of two to three feet and produces five or more eggplants. As the plant matures, it generally needs staking to keep the growing fruit off the ground. It is possible to get two crops from a plant during the growing season: the first crop in July, the second just before frost.

If you are thinking about growing eggplant in a home garden, check with the nearest Extension Service office or the Ministry of Agriculture. They can supply you with detailed information about the varieties most likely to succeed in your area, fertilizing methods and how to deal with insects and plant blights that attack eggplant.

The Standard Varieties

There are four standard varieties of full-size eggplant. In appearance they look alike: large, egg-shaped or somewhat pear-shaped, with a shiny dark purple color. These standard varieties differ primarily in how long it takes for the plants to mature and their resistance to plant diseases.

The quickest growing variety is called the Classic. This variety takes 76 days to mature. The fruit is glossy dark purple-black and long and tapering to the stem. It generally gives two crops during the growing season.

Another quick growing variety is the Midnite, averaging 77 days to maturity. It too is dark purple and has deep oval fruit which grow on tall plants with strong stems. It has been bred to be resistant to many plant diseases that attack eggplant.

Perhaps the most popular is the Black Beauty. This is an old variety that takes 80 days to mature. It has a bushy, low growing plant and its dark purple fruit is oval.

The slowest growing variety is the Special Hibush which takes 85 days to mature. It has dark purple fruit, and is long and tapering toward the stem. The plant is strong and upright and keeps the fruit off the ground.

The Specialty Varieties

The five specialty varieties differ from that of the standard varieties in size, shape and color. Ichiban is an oriental variety that takes 66 days to mature. It is dark purple, tubular, and grows up to 12 inches in length.

Little Fingers and Longtom mature in an average of 68 days and produce smooth slender purple fruit, 4 to 7 inches long. They may remind you of purple cucumbers. Casper is distinguished by its ivory white color. Its medium size fruit mature in 70 days and grow 6 inches long. Most unusual of all is the Italian Pink Bicolor. It is a large bell-shaped fruit, 6 to 8 inches long, with a creamy white base and rose-pink vertical stripes.

The Eggplant Has Five Parts

The stem is the green, spiney top. It is never eaten. Sometimes the eggplant is cooked with the stem, but it is then discarded.

The sepal is the small, coin-like white or brown whorl at the base of the eggplant. It is usually discarded before preparation. However, particularly in recipes using tiny eggplants, the sepal is retained and eaten.

The skin is the outer covering of the eggplant. Most varieties have dark purple skin but the skin may also be white, red or yellowish. The skin may be retained and eaten, or discarded, depending on the recipe.

The pulp or flesh is the white or cream-colored part of the cut eggplant. It is located beneath the skin. The raw pulp, like the raw potato, must be cooked, baked, fried or marinated before eating.

The seeds are usually located in the bottom section of the cut eggplant, although sometimes they appear throughout the plant. They may be brown, or white or a combination of both in one plant. Because seeds in an eggplant are small, numerous and difficult to discard, they are prepared and eaten along with the pulp.

Selecting An Eggplant

In shopping, choose eggplants that have an even shape, with a glossy, smooth skin and a fresh looking green stem. Avoid those eggplants with dark spots on the skin, which indicate decay. Holding the eggplant in your palm; choose one that feels firm and heavy.

To test for ripeness, push gently with your thumb; it should feel firm, not spongy. Some eggplant mavens claim that they can tell whether an eggplant tastes particularly bitter by looking for narrow red and white stripes that radiate out from the stem. Such eggplants are relatively rare; there is no definitive opinion as to whether this is a sign of bitterness.

To retard decay, do not wash eggplants before storing them in the refrigerator. I store my eggplants in ordinary plastic bags, tightly closed. If necessary, eggplant can be safely stored in the refrigerator for up to two weeks, but I believe they taste better if used as soon after harvesting as possible. (An exception: fresh eggplant which is frozen. That can be safely stored for up to a year.) Note: although eggplant is stored unwashed, it should be washed thoroughly before you cook it.

Look For Canned Eggplant

Large supermarkets often stock three types of canned eggplant products. Eggplant slices or cubes, cooked in tomato sauce with Italian or Middle Eastern seasonings can be served as a side vegetable, as topping for pasta, rice or gnocchi, or added to a stew to enhance it.

Canned eggplant puree is another product. It is generally made without seasoning. I have used canned puree in our soup recipes which call for pureed eggplant: Eggplant Yogurt Soup, Quick 'n Easy Carrot Soup, Tomato Eggplant Soup. You can also add the eggplant puree to other packaged soups for a welcome new taste treat.

Also look for pickled baby eggplant, sold in cans or glass jars. These eggplants range in size from one to two inches. The pickling process turns them and the pickle juice red. Eat these eggplants as you would any pickle, whole or sliced, in salads, as a side relish, as an antipasto ingredient. Once opened, the canned eggplants and their pickling juice should be transferred to a glass or non-reactive storage container and stored in the refrigerator. Like any pickle, they can be stored indefinitely.

Nutritional Factors

Eggplant is an excellent source of important nutrients, according to the USDA database on common foods. The following table compares the nutrient profiles for 100 grams each of cooked eggplant and potatoes. Both vegetables are low in fat and cholesterol. In addition, eggplant has more dietary fiber, calcium, vitamin A and folacin than the potato.

Comparison: 100 Grams Cooked Eggplant vs Potato

Nutrient	Eggplant	Potato	Nutrient	Eggplant	Potato
Calories	28.0	87.0	Calcium (mg)	6.0	5.0
Total fat (g)	0.2	0.1	Iron (mg)	0.3	0.3
Saturated fat (g)	0.0	0.0	Vitamin A (iu)	64.0	0.0
Cholesterol (mg)	0.0	0.0	Vitamin B1 (mg)	0.07	0.10
Carbohydrate (g)	6.6	20.1	Vitamin B2 (mg)	0.02	0.02
Dietary fiber (g)	2.5	1.8	Vitamin B6 (mg)	0.08	0.29
Protein (g)	0.8	1.8	Vitamin B12 (mcg)	0.0	0.0
Sodium (mg)	3.0	4.0	Vitamin C (mg)	1.3	13.0
Potassium (mg)	248.0	379.0	Folacin (mcg)	14.4	10.0

How To Plan For Serving Sizes

According to the USDA's Dietary Guidelines, a ½ cup of a cooked vegetable comprises a single adult serving. A 1 pound (455 gr) eggplant, trimmed of stalk and sepal, diced and cooked, yields about four heaping ½ cup servings. Therefore, 1 pound eggplant, prepared as a side vegetable, should serve four adults. Use the following table as a guide when you are preparing eggplant as a side vegetable.

Eggplant Size	Ounces	Grams	Adult Servings
tiny	under 4	under 115	1
small	4-10	115-285	2
medium	10-14	285-395	3
large	14-16	395-455	4
extra large	over 16	over 455	5+

In other types of recipes, the same 1 pound (455 gr) eggplant produces a different yield. Example: in a recipe for a eggplant dip used as an appetizer, the eggplant is roasted and the pulp pureed, yielding approximately 1 cup of puree before any other seasonings are added. Therefore, in each recipe note carefully the weight of eggplant required for the number of servings produced.

Keeping The Eggplant From Turning Dark

Like avocados, fresh uncooked eggplant turns dark when cut and exposed to the air. To minimize this darkening, follow these steps:

1. Use a stainless steel knife to cut the eggplant.

2. When possible, cut the eggplant last when preparing a recipe.

3. If the recipe does not call for salting the eggplant before cooking, place the cut pieces in cold water. This helps keep the eggplant white.

4. When using only part of an eggplant, rub some lemon juice over the unused cut end, cover it tightly with plastic wrap and tie with a rubber band. Refrigerate.

5. Cooking eggplant in stainless steel, enamel, pottery or glass cookware minimizes darkening. Other metal cookware (aluminum, iron, etc) contributes to darkening. However, this does not affect the taste or quality of the food.

Salting The Eggplant

Many recipes call for the cut raw eggplant to be salted prior to cooking. In my experience, salting is helpful because salted eggplant becomes softened and more easily absorbs other flavors in the recipe.

Another reason for salting is suggested by those cooks who maintain that raw eggplant tastes bitter. They recommend salting to draw out the bitter juices. However, I don't agree that all eggplants taste bitter and see no reason to salt for this purpose.

Two methods of salting: salt is spread on the cut pieces which are placed in a colander and left to drain. Or the cut eggplant is cooked in boiling salted water with lemon juice, for 10-15 minutes or until the eggplant is very tender.

How To Freeze Fresh Eggplant

Freezing fresh eggplant saves money and time. Buy eggplant at the height of the summer season when prices are low and freeze slices, cubes or puree. Then, after defrosting, you save preparation time in using these forms of eggplant in recipes.

For freezing, choose eggplants which are glossy and have a uniform color without any brown spots. They should be firm to the touch. Process on the day harvested or bought. Do not process if the eggplant is over-mature. The fresher the vegetable to be frozen, the better the final result.

Freezing Eggplant Slices or Cubes

1. Process one pound of eggplant at a time. Add 4½ teaspoons (23 ml) citric acid or ½ cup (120 ml) lemon juice to 1 gallon (3800 ml) of water. Bring to a boil.
2. While water is coming to the boil, prepare eggplant. Wash and peel eggplant. For slices: slice ½ inch (1.25 cm) thick. For cubes: cut eggplant into ¾ inch (2 cm) cubes.
3. Add eggplant slices\cubes to boiling water. Scald 4 minutes.
4. Lower heat. Remove eggplant slices\cubes with slotted spoon. Cool quickly to stop the cooking process by immersing eggplant slices\cubes in ice water or in the coldest water you have available. Do not cool in water longer than 4 minutes. Drain well. Pat dry with paper towels.
5. Place a sheet of aluminum foil on a cookie sheet. Spread eggplant slices/cubes on the foil and place in freezer.
6A: For slices:
    as soon as they are frozen (within 1 hour), remove slices from foil. Place freezer

wrap or wax paper between the slices. Wrap in freezer paper, heavy duty aluminum foil or seal in plastic freezer boxes. With boxes, leave ½ inch (1.25 cm) headroom for expansion. Seal, label and store in freezer.

6B. For cubes:

as soon as they are frozen, remove from aluminum foil. Pack in heavy duty zip-lock or regular plastic bags suitable for freezing or in freezer jars or plastic freezer boxes. With bags, press out the air before closing, taking care not to crush the cubes. If using freezer jars or boxes, leave ½ inch (1.25 cm) headroom for expansion. Seal, label and store in freezer.

To process a second pound of eggplant: at step 1, add water to the scald bath to bring it back in volume to 1 gallon. Add about half as much citric acid (2 teaspoons \ 10 ml) or ¼ cup (60 ml) lemon juice. Bring water to boil. Go to step 2.

Note: The freezing process adds moisture to the eggplant slices and cubes, making them heavy with water when defrosted. Therefore, defrost frozen eggplant slices and cubes in a colander and pat dry with paper towels before using in a recipe.

Freezing Eggplant Puree

1. Use one of the Basic Roast Eggplant methods. (See page 172)
2. Peel eggplant. Mash well or puree in food processor. Do not add seasoning.
3. Pack into half-pint (240 ml) sterilized freezer jars or heavy-duty zip-lock or plastic bags suitable for freezing. With bags, press out all the air possible before closing. Label.
4. Keep on counter until cool. Place in freezer.

Fourteen Ways Of Preparing Eggplant

There are 14 different ways to prepare eggplant. Which method is chosen depends on the recipe.

1. Basic Roast Eggplant: There are three ways to produce a roasted eggplant – although strictly speaking, one of the methods below involves baking, rather than roasting. In all three methods, the eggplant is kept whole. The eggplant is cooked until it is very soft and tender and the skin is charred. After roasting it is peeled and chopped or pureed.
a) Roasted: cooked over an open flame on a stove top or BBQ grill
b) Roasted: cooked under an open flame in a gas oven grill
c) Baked: pieced twice with a sharp knife and placed in a hot oven

In the following methods of preparation, the eggplant is first cut to the shape required by the recipe.

2. Deep Frying: The eggplant is immersed in a large amount of hot oil.

3. Pan Frying: This methods uses a small amount of oil in a fry pan and the eggplant is sauteed.

4. Oven frying: The bottom of a shallow baking dish is covered with oil. The cut eggplant is first basted with a marinade and/or covered in crumbs of bread, corn meal or cereal, and baked in an oven until tender.

5. Grilling or Broiling: The cut eggplant is seasoned or marinated and placed on a pre-heated grid, either on a BBQ grill or under an open flame in a gas oven grill.

6. Steaming: The eggplant, either whole or cut, is placed in a dish or pan over boiling water, but not in it. The pot of boiling water is covered tightly and the eggplant is steamed until it is tender.

7. Boiling: The cut eggplant is immersed in boiling water until tender.

8. Blanching: This method is used when the eggplant is being prepared for freezing. Similar to boiling, the cut eggplant is immersed in boiling water, but is allowed to cook for only 4 minutes before being removed and cooled.

9. Baking: The cut eggplant is cooked in an oven, in a container that may be covered, or uncovered.

10. Braising: The cut eggplant is cooked covered in a small amount of liquid over low heat on top of the stove or in a low-medium oven. The eggplant may be briefly sauteed before adding liquid.

11. Stewed: Similar to Braising, this method requires the eggplant to simmer in a small quantity of liquid.

12. Stir-frying: This is an oriental method of cooking small pieces of eggplant in a small amount of hot oil over high heat, while stirring constantly.

13. En Papillote: Either paper or aluminum foil is tightly wrapped around the cut eggplant which is then baked until tender.

14. Marinating: The eggplant is not cooked, but soaked in a flavored liquid mixture of an acid, such as wine, vinegar or lemon juice, oil and spices. The marinade is designed to tenderize and flavor the eggplant. This method is used to make eggplant pickles or to use as an ingredient in salads.

Nine All Eggplant Meals

Just for fun, serve an all-eggplant meal to surprise and delight family and friends. Listed below are suggested menus, based on recipes in this book. You will discover that most people cannot tell that each dish contains eggplant.

All American

Tomato Eggplant Soup

Baked Eggplant Fingers

Hobo Stew

Chocolate Eggplant Drop Cookies

Greek

Lentil, Meat and Eggplant Soup

Greek Meatloaf

Rice and Eggplant Pilav

Candied Eggplant

Israeli

Mock Chopped Liver on Crackers

Chauchouka

Crispy Chips

Eggplant Skins over Ice Cream

Indian

Quick and Easy Carrot and Eggplant Soup

Indian Eggplant and Chicken Casserole

Brown Rice Pilav

Tamarind Beverage with No-Oil Muffins

Italian

Minestrone

Caponata

Italian Beef Stew

Chocolate Eggplant Drop Cookies

Middle Eastern

Eggplant Yogurt Soup

Mellawah Eggplant Pie

Tirtzah's Eggplant Salad

Coconut, Raisins & Eggplant Muffins

Mexican

Gazpacho

Salsa Cruda With Eggplant

Spicy Beefy Chili

Melted Eggplant Preserves Over
   Grapefruit Halves

French

Cheese "Sandwiches"

Ratatouille

Fish Stew Provencale

Mock Pumpkin Mousse

Oriental

Chinese Sesame Eggplant Salad

Hunan Style Eggplant

Stir Fried Shrimp and Vegetables with Rice Noodles

Baked Apple Topped with Eggplant Marmalade

Measurement Equivalents

L isted below are the Standard U.S. and Metric unit measurements for volume and weights used in our recipes. For ease of use, the measures are rounded to the nearest whole number.

We also provide a table of oven temperatures in Fahrenheit (F.) and Celsius (C.) Shown too is the Mark number system for showing oven temperatures which is used by many ovens of European manufacture.

Measures of Volume

Standard U.S.	Metric Units	Fluid Ounces
1 teaspoon	5 ml.	1/6 fluid ounce
1/2 tablespoon	7.5 ml.	1/4 fluid ounce
1 tablespoon	15 ml.	1/2 fluid ounce
1/2 cup	120 ml.	4 fluid ounces
1 cup	240 ml	8 fluid ounces

Measures of Weight

Ounces	Pounds	Grams
4	1/4 lb.	115
6	3/8 lb.	170
8	1/2 lb.	225
10	5/8 lb.	285
12	3/4 lb.	340
14	7/8 lb.	395
16	1 lb.	455
32	2 lbs.	905
35 (approx)	2.2 lbs	1000 (kilo)

Oven Temperatures

Fahrenheit	Celsius	Mark
275	140	1
300	150	2
325	160	3
350	180	4
375	190	5
400	200	6
425	220	7
450	230	8
475	245	9

About The Recipes

1. All recipes contain eggplant as a key ingredient, even when the word "eggplant" does not appear in the title. Eggplant should always be washed carefully before use and, unless the recipe indicates otherwise, the stalk and sepal are removed.

2. All recipes are either my invention or my adaptation of an existing recipe. That is, even when a friend was kind enough to share her favorite eggplant recipe, that was just the starting point. Next followed making the recipe in my kitchen and testing the results with friends and family. Invariably, after testing the recipe, I made changes in the ingredients and/or their amounts. Often there were three or four tests before I found the combination which won my family's unqualified approval.

3. Before starting to prepare a recipe, always read it through. All ingredients are listed in order of their use in the preparatory steps. Note that our recipes reduce the amount of fat to a minimum without sacrificing flavor.

4. The recipes show both U.S. standard and metric designations for weights and measures. Use whichever system is more familiar to you. All measures are level except where indicated.

5. A certain leeway is permissible in the weights of ingredients. That is, if the recipe calls for one pound of eggplant, one may use an eggplant that weighs slightly less or more. However, the first time one makes a new recipe, we suggest that you follow the instructions as indicated. If you make significant changes in ingredients or seasonings, the finished product is likely to be quite different from the dish described in the recipe.

6. Experienced cooks know that even if one follows a recipe carefully, the result may be off the mark because of differences in utensils and stoves. Even altitude may be a significant factor in how a recipe turns out.

7. Only after you have tested a recipe, following instructions, should you feel free to make any adjustments in ingredients or cooking times to suit your own taste. This is certainly permissible and even desirable because, in the last analysis, cooking is a creative process.

8. For the convenience of those households which keep a kosher kitchen, each recipe indicates clearly whether it is dairy, parve or meat. The designation appears to the right of the name of the recipe.

9. For recipes which specify an ingredient marked "parve", such as chicken or beef soup powder: if you cannot find the item labelled "parve", substitute a vegetarian chicken or beef flavored soup powder, usually available in health food stores.

* * *

Appetizers & Salads

Baba Ghanoush

Parve
Makes about 1 cup

1 pound (455 gr) eggplant, roasted. See page 172 for Basic Roast Eggplant recipe. Use open flame method.

3 cloves garlic, minced

¼ teaspoon salt

2 tablespoons lemon juice

2 tablespoons tehina paste

¼ teaspoon cumin

pinch ground hot red pepper (cayenne pepper)

paprika

1 tablespoon snipped parsley

pitted black olives, sliced

❶ **G**rill eggplant according to Basic Roast Eggplant recipe, but omit the lemon juice, salt and pepper indicated in that recipe.

❷ **M**ash by hand, or in a food processor, the eggplant, garlic, salt, lemon juice, tehina paste, cumin, and hot red pepper.

❸ **R**emove to a serving dish. Garnish with paprika, parsley and sliced olives. Cover. Refrigerate and allow to cool before serving.

Note:

Mix well the tehina paste in its container to combine the paste and natural oils before measuring.

This traditional Middle East eggplant puree was given to me by Edith Grunbaumn who worked her salad magic for many years in the kitchen of Kibbutz Sde Boker, in Israel's Negev Desert. (This is the kibbutz where David Ben Gurion, Israel's first Prime Minister, retired. Visitors can tour the house where he and his wife Paula spent their last years.)
Baba Ghanoush is rich and creamy with a pleasant lemony-smoky flavor. Serve it as a dip or in a sandwich with fresh vegetables. Feel free to vary the flavors of the ingredients according to taste.

Caponata

Parve
Serves 4-5 as a warm side dish
Serves 6-8 as a cold relish

1 heaping cup cubed peeled
  eggplant, cut ¼ inch (0.64 cm)

2 teaspoons olive oil

4 teaspoons vegetable oil

1 medium onion, chopped

1 sweet red pepper, diced

1 cup sliced celery

⅓ cup thickly sliced fresh
  mushroom caps

1 cup cauliflower florets

½ pound (225 gr) ripe plum
  tomatoes, diced

1 teaspoon cornstarch

6 green pitted olives, chopped

6 black pitted olives, chopped

2 tablespoons red wine vinegar

1 teaspoon sugar

1 teaspoon dried basil

❶ Lightly salt eggplant cubes. Set aside to drain.

❷ In a large fry pan, preferably non-stick, add olive
oil and 2 teaspoons vegetable oil over moderate
heat. Saute onion, pepper, celery, mushrooms,
cauliflower florets and tomatoes about
10 minutes. Remove vegetables from pan and
reserve. Remove pan from heat.

❸ Dry eggplant with paper towels. Return pan to
heat and add 2 teaspoons vegetable oil. Add
eggplant cubes and immediately sprinkle
cornstarch over eggplant. Saute about 5 minutes
until golden.

❹ Mix in reserved vegetables, olives, wine vinegar,
sugar and basil and cook briefly. Store in a glass
container in the refrigerator.
Serve cold.

Caponata is a versatile Italian salad you will want to keep on hand. It can be served in many ways: as a salsa, an appetizer, an antipasto ingredient, as a colorful dish in a buffet, or as a vegetable side dish.

Chinese Sesame Eggplant Salad

Parve
Makes about 2 cups

1¼ pounds (570 gr.) roasted eggplant. See page 172 for Basic Roast Eggplant recipe. Use oven method.

1 tablespoon salad oil

1½ tablespoons sesame seeds

1 teaspoon minced garlic

1 teaspoon minced ginger root

1 tablespoon soy sauce

1 tablespoon vinegar

½ teaspoon sugar

2 green onions, whites and greens, chopped ¼ in. (0.64 cm.)

❶ When roasted eggplant is cool enough to handle, remove stalk and peel off skin of eggplant. Tear pulp into shreds, discarding any large seed pockets. Over a strainer, rinse the shredded eggplant in cold water and allow to drain at least 30 minutes, pressing water out gently.

❷ While eggplant is draining, heat oil in a small fry pan. Add sesame seeds and saute over low heat about 2 minutes, until golden. Remove from pan and reserve.

❸ While pan is still hot, stir in garlic and ginger root. Saute briefly. Remove from pan. Cool.

❹ In a small bowl, combine soy sauce, vinegar and sugar. Stir in the sesame seeds, and garlic-ginger root mixture.

❺ Combine drained eggplant, sesame spices mixture and green onions. Mix well. Cover and store in refrigerator.
Serve cold.

You need not wait until you serve a Chinese meal to make this salad, as it also goes well with broiled meats and fish. The preparation can be done in advance and assembled at the last moment.

Crispy Chips

½ cup white flour

½ teaspoon sweet paprika

1 teaspoon baking powder

dash salt

½ cup water

1½ tablespoons olive oil

1 egg, beaten

1 teaspoon dried zaytar or oregano.

1 small (8 ounces \ 225 gr) eggplant. See Note.

1 cup or more of vegetable oil

❶ **I**n a medium bowl, blend together the flour, paprika, baking powder, and salt. Whisk in the water, olive oil and beaten egg until you have a smooth mixture. Add the zaytar or oregano and stir until well mixed. Cover and allow to stand while you prepare the eggplant.

❷ **W**ash eggplant. Dry skin. Cut in half lengthwise. With the skin side up, cut ¼ inch (0.64 cm) slices to make half moons. Place a cake cooling rack on a baking sheet and place it near the stove. Or, attach a draining rack to a wok. Line a large plate with paper towels and keep it nearby.

❸ **I**n a wok or deep fry pan, heat oil until a very small piece of eggplant immediately begins to sizzle. The oil should be deep enough for the eggplant to float on top.

❹ **W**ith metal tongs or chopsticks, dip a slice of eggplant in the batter, pressing down to cover. Shake off excess batter. Drop it into the hot oil. Fry 30 seconds, turn and fry until golden. Remove and drain first on cake cooling rack, or wok draining rack, then on paper towels. Working quickly, continue the process with all the other slices. You should be able to fry 4-6 slices at at time. (Refrigerate extra batter to make more Crispy Chips or use it to prepare flavorful crepes.)

Note:
If a small eggplant is unavailable, use the bottom half of a larger one.

❺ **S**erve hot or at room temperature. Reheat, if desired, at 400 F (200 C \ gas mark 6) until crisp or deep fry again briefly

*T*his recipe comes from Reuven Kanias, who runs a kiosk in Mitzpe Ramon. He serves three or four of these batter fried eggplant slices in a pita, with falafel and salads. I've adapted his large quantities to family size. I serve them heaped on a platter as an appetizer or vegetable. It is hard to tell how many this recipe serves because they go so fast. In fact, I have to restrain myself while I'm frying them not to eat them all.

Curried Eggplant Salad

1 medium (10 ounces \ 285 gr) eggplant, peeled, cut in ½ inch (1.25 cm) cubes

1 tablespoon olive oil

1 tablespoon vegetable oil

3 tablespoons French onion soup mix

1 tablespoon dried dill

¼ teaspoon curry powder

¼ teaspoon cumin

dash white pepper

1 teaspoon lemon juice

3 heaping tablespoons mayonnaise

❶ **A**dd eggplant cubes to heated olive and vegetable oils. Stir to coat. Add French onion soup mix, and dried dill. Cover. Cook on low heat for 10 minutes, stirring occasionally.

❷ **S**tir in curry powder, cumin, white pepper and lemon juice. Cook 1-2 minutes. Cool slightly.

❸ **S**tir in mayonnaise. Store covered in the refrigerator for several hours before serving.

This is a quick, spicy salad which uses a packaged soup mix for its rich onion flavor. Serve it as a sandwich spread with lettuce and tomatoes or as a dip with taco chips or celery stalks.

Delmonico Salad

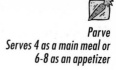

Parve
Serves 4 as a main meal or
6-8 as an appetizer

8 ounces (225 gr) eggplant, peeled, cubed ½ inch (1.25 cm)

½ cup white wine vinegar

⅓ cup water

1 medium onion, chopped

1 large grapefruit

1 can (7.5 ounces \ 213 gr) salmon in natural juice, drained

¼ cup bottled chili sauce

½ cup mayonnaise

❶ **I**n a glass or ceramic bowl, combine cubed eggplant, white wine vinegar, water and chopped onion. Cover. Refrigerate 2-4 hours. Toss occasionally.

❷ **P**eel grapefruit. Remove membranes. Slice in ½ inch (1.25 cm) thick crosswise slices, then cut grapefruit slices in segments.

❸ **R**emove bones and skin from drained salmon. Flake.

❹ **D**rain cubed eggplant and chopped onion, reserving marinade.

❺ **I**n a large bowl, combine drained cubed eggplant, chopped onion, grapefruit segments and drained flaked salmon.

❻ **I**n a small bowl, combine bottled chili sauce and mayonnaise. Add to eggplant, grapefruit and salmon mixture. Mix in.
Serve cold.

Note:
Use reserved marinade in salad dressings or other recipes.

To serve:
On a salad plate, place salad over shredded lettuce. Decorate sides of plate with slices of tomatoes and cucumbers.

Unusual ingredients combine to make an elegant, delicious salad. Serve it for lunch or dinner as a main meal with dark crusty bread, or as a starter.

Eggplant Salad In Lettuce Leaves

Parve
Serves 4

1 cup coarsely chopped roasted eggplant. See page 172 for Basic Roast Eggplant recipe. Use any method.

4 small leaves of romaine lettuce

1 cup washed and coarsely chopped lettuce

1 tablespoon plus 1 teaspoon red wine vinegar

2 cloves garlic, minced

1 heaping tablespoon snipped fresh parsley

Tobasco sauce to taste

salt and pepper to taste

2 teaspoons olive oil

4 pitted black olives, sliced

❶ **P**repare 1 cup of roasted eggplant as indicated in the basic recipe. Add the lemon juice as indicated in the basic recipe, but omit the salt and pepper. Cover, refrigerate to cool.

❷ **W**ash lettuce leaves and shake off the water. Sprinkle the leaves with 1 teaspoon red wine vinegar. Wrap in paper towels and refrigerate. Separately, cover and refrigerate the chopped lettuce.

❸ **T**o the cooled eggplant, add 1 tablespoon red wine vinegar, minced garlic, parsley, tobasco sauce, salt, pepper and olive oil. Gently mix all together. Cover and refrigerate until ready to serve.

❹ **W**hen ready to serve: place lettuce leaves on individual serving plates. Gently mix the chopped lettuce with the eggplant mixture. Spoon eggplant mixture onto the lettuce leaves. Decorate with sliced olives.
Ready to serve.

Note:
You can substitute canned, or frozen and cooked, artichoke bottoms for the lettuce leaves.
Since artichoke bottoms are quite small, the recipe will serve 6 to 8.

This salad makes a nice first course when served on lettuce leaves. Without the lettuce leaves, the salad can be used as a spread on bread or rice cakes or stuffed in a pita with other ingredients such as falafel, bean sprouts, tomatoes, and/or cooked meats.

Eggplant Puree In Oil

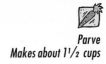

Parve
Makes about 1¹/₂ cups

1 pound (455 gr) eggplant

2 cloves garlic, minced

2 tablespoons lemon juice

1 tablespoon olive oil

salt to taste

black pepper to taste

3 tablespoons chopped fresh
  parsley or coriander (cilantro)
  leaves

ground hot red pepper to taste
  (cayenne powder)

❶ **R**oast eggplant according to one of the methods in the Basic Roast Eggplant recipe (page 172), but omit the salt, pepper and lemon juice in that recipe. Cool and peel eggplant according to recipe.

❷ **C**hop flesh well by hand until smooth, or puree in food processor. Add garlic and lemon juice and slowly add olive oil, stirring, or processing, continually.

❸ **W**hen oil has combined well with eggplant, add salt, black pepper, parsley or coriander and red pepper. Taste and adjust seasonings. Blend well again.

❹ **C**ool in refrigerator. When eggplant puree is cold, taste and adjust seasonings again. Keeps well in refrigerator for several days.

This basic Middle East eggplant salad is another recipe given to me by Edith Grunbaumn of Kibbutz Sde Boker.

Serve this salad as a dip with raw vegetables, in a pita, on a rice cake or slice of bread, or as a side salad. It can be as spicy or as bland as you make it, although it is best with a little "bite" to it. I also prefer the taste of the eggplant when it is roasted in an open flame, but any roasting method will do.

Indian Eggplant Salad

1 pound (455 gr) eggplant, roasted. See page 172 for Basic Roast Eggplant recipe. Use open flame method.

1 medium onion, chopped

¼ teaspoon ground ginger

1 tablespoon plus 1 teaspoon olive oil

½ teaspoon dried coriander leaves, rubbed

½ teaspoon ground cumin

¼ teaspoon turmeric

½ teaspoon garam masala. See Note.

1 teaspoon sugar

2 cloves garlic, minced

1 tablespoon lemon juice

1 cup yogurt

½ teaspoon dried mint, rubbed

¼ teaspoon salt

1-2 tablespoons coarsely snipped parsley

❶ **G**rill, peel and drain eggplant according to Basic Roast Eggplant recipe, but omit the lemon juice, salt and pepper indicated.

❷ **I**n a fry pan, preferably non-stick, fry onion and ginger in 1 teaspoon olive oil until dark golden brown. Add to the onions the coriander, cumin, turmeric, garam masala and sugar and mix in briefly until onions are coated with added spices.

❸ **T**ransfer the grilled eggplant to a food processor. Add fried onion-spice mixture, 1 tablespoon olive oil, garlic, lemon juice, yogurt, mint and salt. Process until eggplant is pureed and spices are well mixed in.

❹ **R**emove to a serving dish. Sprinkle parsley over the top. Cover and refrigerate to cool before serving.

Note:

Garam masala is a mixture of various spices. It can be bought ready-made in Indian markets. If not available in your area, mix your own. See page 174.

This spicy salad produces a lovely golden color, enhanced by the contrasting green of the parsley. It can be served as a cold salad with bread and fresh or pickled vegetables, or serve it warm with curries and pilavs.

Imam Bayildi

2 long thin (each 8-9 ounces \
  225-255 gr) eggplants

¼ cup plus 1 tablespoon olive oil

1 teaspoon sugar

1 tablespoon lemon juice

1 teaspoon salt

¾ cup chopped onions

⅛ teaspoon minced garlic

1 cup diced tomatoes

1 cup firmly packed, finely
  chopped parsley with stems

salt to taste

pepper to taste

❶ **C**ut off stalk and sepal. Cut eggplants in half crosswise. Peel three 1 inch wide lengthwise strips from each eggplant, leaving alternating strips of flesh and peel. Discard peel. Make one deep lengthwise slit down the full length of one strip, without cutting right through the eggplant.

❷ **L**ay the eggplants side by side in a large pot. Pour ¼ cup olive oil over them. Add water to cover. (The eggplants will float). Add sugar, lemon juice and salt. Cover. Bring water to a boil. Lower heat and simmer until eggplant are very soft, about 30-45 minutes. Remove eggplants with a slotted spoon. Drain well.

❸ **W**hile eggplants are simmering, make the filling. In a non-stick fry pan, heat 1 tablespoon olive oil. Add onions and garlic. Saute over low heat 5 minutes.

❹ **R**aise heat to medium. Add tomatoes, parsley, salt and pepper to taste. Saute 10 minutes or more until a thick, jam-like mixture is formed. Remove from heat.

❺ **D**ivide vegetable mixture into 4 equal portions. When drained eggplants are cool enough to handle, spoon mixture into the slit in each eggplant. Gently squeeze closed to keep in filling. Refrigerate covered. Chill at least 1 hour. Serve very cold with the filling side up. Can be prepared a day ahead.

This is the legendary recipe that caused a Turkish clergyman to faint when he found how much precious olive oil went into its preparation. Fortunately, olive oil is affordable today, so no one need be denied this special appetizer.

Eggplant Salad With Mayonnaise

Parve
Makes about 1½ cups

1 pound (455 gr) eggplant, roasted. See page 172 for Basic Roast Eggplant recipe. Use open flame method.

1 tablespoon lemon juice

3 cloves garlic, minced

½ teaspoon salt

4 tablespoons mayonnaise

❶ **M**ash roasted eggplant, or puree in a food processor.

❷ **A**dd all other ingredients and mix well together. Cover. Store in refrigerator until cool. Adjust seasonings to taste.

Note:

It is not necessary to wash off all the charred eggplant particles as small amounts of these enhance the flavor.

*T*his popular eggplant salad is found on restaurant menus all over the Middle East. In Israel, it can also be bought prepared in super markets. The advantage of making your own is that it has no preservatives, and you can adjust the seasonings to your own taste.

This salad gets its special character from its maker. It is possible to use more or less of the lemon juice, garlic, salt and mayonnaise. You can even add pepper or chopped onions if you wish. Serve it as a side salad, as a dip with chips, in a pita, or on a rice cake or slice of bread.

Lebanese Salad

Parve
Serves 4

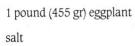

1 pound (455 gr) eggplant

salt

1 small zucchini

3-4 tablespoons olive oil

dash black pepper

½ cup chopped coriander (cilantro) or parsley

3 tablespoons orange juice

1½ lemon juice

salt to taste (optional)

❶ Cut unpeeled eggplant in half lengthwise. Cut each half into ¼ inch (0.64 cm) half-moon slices. Place in a colander. Sprinkle with salt. Allow to stand 15-20 minutes.

❷ Meanwhile, with a vegetable peeler, cut zucchini lengthwise in very thin slices. Reserve.

❸ Rinse eggplant. Pat dry with paper towels. Brush both sides of eggplant lightly with some of the olive oil. Place on a baking tray. Cook under a preheated grill for 3-5 minutes, or until lightly browned on both sides. Cool.

❹ In a bowl, add eggplant, zucchini, remainder of olive oil, black pepper, chopped coriander (cilantro) or parsley, orange and lemon juices. Add salt to taste. Toss gently to combine. Serve cold.

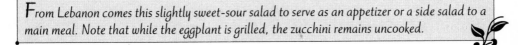

From Lebanon comes this slightly sweet-sour salad to serve as an appetizer or a side salad to a main meal. Note that while the eggplant is grilled, the zucchini remains uncooked.

Marinated Eggplant Pickles

Parve
Serves 4

1 pound (455 gr) eggplant, peeled,
   sliced ¼ inch (0.64 cm)

salt

1 cup white wine vinegar

4-6 cloves garlic, crushed

1 tablespoon dried oregano

vegetable oil

❶ **S**prinkle each slice of eggplant with salt. Arrange in layers in a colander. Allow to drain from 2 to 4 hours. Occasionally gently shake the slices to drain the juices.

❷ **I**n a wide bottom ovenproof glass or ceramic pot, add eggplant slices and vinegar. If necessary, add a little water to cover. Bring to a slow simmer and cook about 10 minutes. Drain well. Reserve the vinegar.

❸ **R**ub oregano between your hands and place in a small bowl.

❹ **W**ith tongs, place eggplant slices in a large sterilized glass jar, putting some garlic pieces and oregano between each layer.

❺ **A**dd oil to cover all the eggplant. Cover jar tightly. Refrigerate. Serve after 1 week.

Note:

Strain and discard the eggplant seeds from the reserved vinegar (Step 2). It can then be used again to prepare another batch of pickles or as an ingredient for a tasty homemade salad dressing. Also, when these pickled eggplants are finished, the oil in the jar can be reused for flavorful salad dressings.

This recipe is quickly assembled. The problem is that the eggplant pickles must marinate for a week before they are ready. But these pickles are so good that they are well worth the wait. They last indefinitely stored in the refrigerator.

Mock Chopped Liver

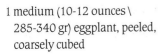

Parve
Makes about 1³/₄ cups

1 medium (10-12 ounces \ 285-340 gr) eggplant, peeled, coarsely cubed

½ pound (225 gr) onions, diced

2 tablespoons margarine

2 hard boiled eggs

1 tablespoon parve chicken soup powder

salt to taste

pepper to taste

❶ **S**alt eggplant cubes and drain in colander for 30 minutes.

❷ **M**eanwhile, saute onions in margarine, for 30 minutes on moderate heat, stirring occasionally.

❸ **R**inse eggplant cubes in cold water. Drain and squeeze out moisture.

❹ **A**dd eggplant to onions. Saute about 5 minutes. Cover. Lower heat. Cook for 20 to 30 minutes, stirring occasionally, until eggplant is very soft.

❺ **R**emove to a chopping bowl. Add hard boiled eggs, chicken soup powder, salt and pepper to taste and chop very fine. Or put mixture with eggs into a food processor and puree. Refrigerate. When cold, taste and adjust seasonings.

This makes a nice first course appetizer when placed on lettuce leaves topped with a radish rose. Alternatively, use as canapes with crackers, and cucumber circles, or stuffed in celery sticks. It tastes like the 'real thing' without all the extra calories to be found in liver.

Pureed Eggplant With Yogurt

1 pound (455 gr) eggplant, roasted. See page 172 for Basic Roast Eggplant recipe. Use open flame method.

1 tablespoon olive oil

2 cloves garlic, minced

1 tablespoon lemon juice

1 cup yogurt

½ teaspoon dried mint

¼ teaspoon salt

1 tablespoon snipped fresh parsley

❶ **G**rill eggplant according to Basic Roast Eggplant recipe, but omit the lemon juice, salt and pepper indicated.

❷ **M**ash grilled eggplant by hand, or puree in food processor. Add olive oil, garlic, lemon juice, yogurt, dried mint and salt and process until smooth.

❸ **R**emove to a serving dish. Sprinkle parsley over the top. Cover and refrigerate to cool before serving.

This relatively bland-tasting salad is very traditional in Arab cookery. Use it as a dip with falafel balls, fresh vegetables, or to stuff in a pita. It is also good over a rice cake, topped with a slice of tomato.

Salsa Cruda With Eggplant

Parve
Makes about 5 cups

½ pound (225 gr) eggplant, peeled and diced

½ cup red wine vinegar

⅓ cup water

1 medium onion, sliced

1½ pounds (680 gr) fresh tomatoes, plum or regular, cut in chunks

1 rib celery, finely chopped

2 fresh green chili peppers, chopped

1 teaspoon salt

¼ cup fresh coriander (cilantro) leaves

¼ cup olive oil

❶ In a glass bowl, combine diced eggplant with red wine vinegar and water. Lay sliced onions over top. Cover. Marinate in refrigerator for 2 to 4 hours.

❷ After marinating time, remove sliced onions and reserve. Drain eggplant. Reserve the marinade.

❸ In a food processor, add reserved sliced onions, tomatoes, celery, chili peppers, salt, coriander leaves and olive oil. Process about 20 to 30 seconds until vegetables have been reduced to small pieces, but not pureed. Remove to a large bowl.

❹ Add drained diced eggplant and 2 tablespoons of the reserved marinade. Mix together. Cover and refrigerate several hours until ready to serve. Keeps at least a week in the refrigerator.

Notes:

A: To make the recipe by hand: at Step 3, dice the tomatoes and green chili peppers and chop fine the fresh coriander leaves. Remove to large bowl. Add the reserved sliced onion, salt and olive oil. Mix. Continue with Step 4.
B: The extra reserved marinade can be used as an ingredient in homemade salad dressing.

Salsa is a versatile Mexican sauce. It is used as a topping over bean or meat tacos, as a condiment with egg dishes, and as a relish or salad with main meals. There are actually many different salsas. Some are made from vegetables and fruits, such as pineapple and papaya, and range in pungency from mild to very hot. This recipe produces a mild salsa, good in a pita with meat or fresh vegetables. It is quickly made in a food processor, but we have also included directions for making it by hand. See Note A.

Tirtzah's Eggplant Salad

Parve
Makes about 1¹/₂ cups

1 very large onion (or 2 medium), chopped

2-3 tablespoons olive oil

1 pound (455 gr) eggplant, peeled, diced

1 tablespoon parve chicken soup powder

1 tablespoon honey

1 tablespoon dried dill

mayonnaise (optional)

❶ **F**ry onions in oil until slightly browned.

❷ **A**dd diced eggplant, stir in briefly.

❸ **A**dd parve chicken soup powder, honey, and dill and stir in. Cover pan. Cook on a very low flame until eggplant is soft, about 15-20 minutes. Stir occasionally. Do not add any liquid because eggplant releases its juices to provide the necessary moisture.

❹ **R**emove from pot. Keep in a covered dish in the refrigerator until ready to serve.

❺ **I**f desired, just before serving, add 1 tablespoon mayonnaise only to the portion you are serving. Keep remainder of eggplant mixture covered in the refrigerator, adding mayonnaise only when ready to serve.

This heavenly recipe comes from my friend Tirtzah Steckel of Netanya, Israel, who generously shared it with me. While the recipe calls for the addition of mayonnaise, I find it is just as tasty without it, which also helps to cut calories.

Piccalilli Eggplant Salad

Parve
Makes 4 cups

1 pound (455 gr) eggplant, unpeeled, cubed ½ inch (1.25 cm)

1 tablespoon olive oil

1 tablespoon vegetable oil

2 cups canned crushed tomatoes with juice

½ cup prepared piccalilli

❶ **S**alt eggplant cubes. Allow to stand for 15 minutes. Pat dry with paper towels.

❷ **H**eat olive oil and vegetable oil in a medium pot. Add eggplant cubes. Fry over medium heat, stirring until softened, about 10 minutes.

❸ **A**dd tomatoes with juice. Cover. Lower heat. Cook about 30 minutes, stirring occasionally. Remove from heat. Cool 15 minutes.

❹ **S**tir in piccalilli. Transfer to a container. Refrigerate. Serve cold.

This tangy, quickly prepared salad can be served on a bed of lettuce as an appetizer or as a cold side vegetable that goes well with any meal.

Soup Recipes

Gazpacho –
A Cold Vegetable Soup

6 ounces (170 gr) eggplant, peeled, diced

1 large tomato, chopped

1 1/2 cups tomato juice

1 cucumber, chopped

1 medium onion, chopped

1 large green pepper, finely diced

1 small fresh green chili pepper, finely diced

2 cloves garlic, minced

2 tablespoons vegetable oil

1-2 tablespoon vinegar

1 teaspoon salt

1/8 teaspoon black pepper

❶ **P**arboil diced eggplant 3-5 minutes. Drain well, squeeze dry.

❷ **C**ombine eggplant and all other ingredients in a large bowl.

❸ **C**over and chill in refrigerator until ready to serve.

To Prepare in a Food Processor:

❶ **P**arboil diced eggplant 3-5 minutes. Drain well, squeeze dry.

❷ **C**oarsely cut tomato, cucumber, onion, green pepper, and chili pepper. Add to the food processor with 1/2 cup tomato juice. Add diced eggplant. Process until vegetables are well chopped, but not pureed.

❸ **R**emove vegetables to a large bowl. Add remaining 1 cup tomato juice. Cover and chill in refrigerator until ready to serve.

Tip:

In a hurry to serve the Gazpacho and have no time to chill it? Simply add an ice cube to each serving for several minutes. Remove ice cube before serving.

Gazpacho is a popular Mexican soup, with more vegetables than soup. It is ideal to serve on hot "dog days." If you have a food processor you can make it even more quickly. (See special instructions above.) The recipe doubles nicely, so you can make more to keep on hand. Serve with bread croutons or packaged tortilla snacks. It goes well with any warm weather meal.

Quick And Easy Carrot & Eggplant Soup

4 medium carrots, thinly sliced (about 1 heaping cup)

1 small (8 ounces \ 225 gr) eggplant, peeled, cubed 1 inch (2.5 cm)

3 cups water

2 tablespoons parve chicken soup powder

¼ teaspoon dried mint, rubbed

1 heaping tablespoon dried fried onion flakes

❶ **I**n a large pot, add all ingredients except onion flakes. Bring to a boil. Lower heat and cook until eggplant is tender and carrots are soft.

❷ **W**ith a slotted spoon, remove carrots and eggplant. Remove ½ cup of liquid. Add to food processor or blender and process until a thick pulp is formed. (Can also be mashed by hand.)

❸ **R**eturn to soup pot. Stir in onion flakes. Serve hot or cold. Stir well before serving.

This tasty soup is appropriate whatever the weather. On a wintry day, it can be served hot to warm you — or in the summertime, served cold, it is a perfect cooler. I always make extra servings which I freeze for later use.

Minestrone Eggplant Soup

1 tablespoon olive oil

½ pound (225 gr) boneless beef, cut in ½ inch (1.25 cm) cubes

½ medium onion, chopped

1 clove garlic, minced

¾ cup diced carrots

½ cup chopped celery, plus some fresh celery leaves

½ heaping cup diced zucchini

2 cups cubed peeled eggplant, cut ½ inch (1.25 cm)

6 cups hot beef stock or 6 cups boiling water and 2 tablespoons beef soup powder

⅛ teaspoon pepper

½ teaspoon dried oregano

½ teaspoon dried basil

½ teaspoon coriander (cilantro) leaves

½ cup cooked chick peas (garbanzo beans) or canned, drained. See Note.

½ cup diced fresh plum tomatoes

½ cup uncooked macaroni

❶ **I**n a large pot, heat olive oil. Add beef and brown on all sides on high heat.

❷ **L**ower heat slightly and add onions and garlic. Saute until onions are golden.

❸ **A**dd all other ingredients except chick peas, tomatoes and macaroni. Bring back to a boil, cover and simmer 30 to 45 minutes until meat is soft.

❹ **A**dd chick peas, tomatoes and macaroni and cook uncovered another 15 to 20 minutes. Serve hot.

To cook chick peas with quick-soak method

❶ **S**ort and wash ¼ cup chick peas. Place in a pot with 1½ cups water, ⅛ teaspoon salt and ½ teaspoon oil.

❷ **B**ring to a boil and cook 2 minutes. Remove pot from heat and let stand 1 hour. Return to heat. Bring to a boil. Lower heat and simmer chick peas about 1½ hours or more, until tender. (Chick peas never get really soft.)

*T*his soup is based on an Italian classic. It can be served as the main dish when accompanied with a large salad and slices of toasted garlic Italian bread.

Lentil, Meat & Eggplant Soup

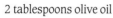

2 tablespoons olive oil

¼ pound (115 gr) boneless beef, cut in ½ inch (1.25) cubes

¼ pound (115 gr) skinless and boneless turkey, cut in ½ inch (1.25 cm) cubes

1 medium onion, sliced in half-rings, separated

2 cups cubed peeled eggplant, cut ½ inch (1.25 cm)

½ cup brown lentils, picked over, well washed, drained

½ cup diced celery

1½ cups diced carrots

4 cups hot chicken stock or 4 cups boiling water and 2 tablespoons chicken soup powder

¼ cup tomato paste

2 cloves garlic, minced

1 teaspoon dried parsley

dash pepper

1 teaspoon turmeric

❶ **I**n a large pot, add 1 tablespoon olive oil. When hot, add beef and turkey and brown on all sides.

❷ **A**dd the remaining tablespoon olive oil, then the onion, eggplant cubes and lentils, stirring and sauteing after each addition until well coated with oil.

❸ **A**dd celery, carrots, chicken stock and tomato paste. Bring stock to the boil. Cover, reduce heat. Simmer about 30 to 45 minutes until meat and carrots are soft. Lentils should be soft, not mushy.

❹ **R**emove from heat. Stir in garlic, parsley, pepper and turmeric. Cover and let the flavors blend for a few minutes before serving.
Serve hot.

This nutritious soup could make a complete protein meal. Serve it with bread, a whole grain, a salad, or cooked vegetables to round out the meal.

Tomato Eggplant Soup

1 pound (455 gr) whole eggplant, with stalk and sepal

3 tablespoons parve beef soup powder and 3 cups water

1 tablespoon onion soup powder

3 cups tomato juice

2 teaspoons worcestershire sauce

1 tablespoon lemon juice

1 bay leaf

black pepper to taste

1 cucumber, very finely chopped

❶ **P**reheat oven to 475 F (245 C \ gas mark 9).

❷ **W**ash and pierce eggplant in several places. Bake until very soft, turning several times. Cool until able to handle. Peel. Mash by hand or puree in food processor.

❸ **M**eanwhile, in a pot, add parve beef soup powder, water, onion soup powder, tomato juice, worcestershire sauce, lemon juice, bay leaf and black pepper. Bring to a boil. Lower flame and simmer 5-10 minutes.

❹ **R**emove from flame. Remove bay leaf.

❺ **A**dd mashed or pureed eggplant. Stir until smooth. Stir in cucumber.
Serve hot or cold.

This is an appealing soup, especially welcome when served cold during hot summer days or when served hot on cold winter evenings. Because most of the ingredients are usually on hand in most kitchens, it can be made quickly and economically.

Eggplant Yogurt Soup

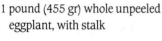

1 pound (455 gr) whole unpeeled eggplant, with stalk

3 tablespoons parve chicken soup powder and 4 cups water

1 tablespoon onion soup powder

1 teaspoon dried basil, rubbed

white or black pepper, freshly ground (to taste)

1 teaspoon flour

1 tablespoon water

1 scant cup yogurt

❶ **P**reheat oven to 400 F (200 C \ gas mark 6)

❷ **W**ash eggplant and pierce it twice. Bake about 45 minutes until very soft, turning several times. Cool until able to handle.

❸ **P**eel the eggplant. Drain the pulp while you prepare the soup.

❹ **B**ring chicken soup powder, water and onion soup powder to a boil. Lower heat and cook for 5 minutes.

❺ **W**hile soup is coming to the boil, puree the eggplant in a food processor or mash very well by hand.

❻ **A**dd basil and pepper to the soup. Add eggplant puree and with a wire whisk, stir until smooth. Cook another 5 minutes.

❼ **R**emove from flame. Cool 4-5 minutes.

❽ **S**tabilize the yogurt: In a medium bowl, mix flour and water. Stir in the yogurt.

❾ **S**lowly add yogurt mixture by spoonfuls as you stir with a wire whisk until smooth. Serve immediately or refrigerate and serve cold.

Note:

Do not reheat else the yogurt may curdle. To prepare ahead, bake the eggplant but do not peel. Reserve until ready to use. Then proceed with the recipe at Step 3.

---

*T*his delicate creamy soup has a smokey flavor that is hard to resist. It needs few ingredients and is easy to make. It is delicious served warm or cold.

Chinese Cabbage Soup

1 tablespoon vegetable oil

1 small onion, chopped

¼ pound (115 gr) eggplant, peeled and diced

6 leaves Chinese cabbage, chopped

4¼ cups (1 liter) canned tomato juice

2 large kaffir leaves.

¼ cup thin rice noodles, cut in 2 inch (5 cm) pieces

❶ **I**n a large soup pot, heat vegetable oil. Add chopped onions and diced eggplant. Fry 2-3 minutes.

❷ **A**dd chopped Chinese cabbage. Fry 1 minute.

❸ **A**dd tomato juice. Place kaffir leaves in a metal tea caddy, or wrap in cheesecloth. Add to pot.

❹ **B**ring tomato juice to a boil. Cover. Lower heat. Simmer for 20 minutes. Remove kaffir leaves and discard.

❺ **A**dd cut up rice noodles. Cook 5 minutes more. Serve hot.

This is a hearty soup for cold winter nights. The kaffir leaves, sold in Indian stores, are optional but I use them because they add an extra tasty piquancy to the soup.

Thai Pumpkin & Eggplant Soup

¼ teaspoon cayenne pepper powder

1 large clove garlic, minced

1 teaspoon minced ginger root

¼ teaspoon dried ground coriander (cilantro)

⅛ teaspoon white pepper

⅛ teaspoon salt

2 teaspoons vegetable oil

1 medium onion, finely chopped

1½ cups peeled pumpkin, cut in bite size chunks

1½ cups peeled eggplant, cut in bite size chunks

2 tablespoons parve chicken soup powder and 4½ cups water

½ cup coconut milk

❶ **C**ombine the first 6 spices in a small bowl.

❷ **H**eat oil in a large soup pot. Add spices and chopped onions. Saute 4 minutes.

❸ **S**tir in pumpkin and eggplant. Add parve chicken soup powder, water and coconut milk.

❹ **B**ring to a boil. Lower heat. Cover. Simmer for 15-20 minutes, until vegetables are just tender. Do not overcook.

❺ **W**ith a slotted spoon, remove all the pumpkin and eggplant. Puree with ½ cup stock in a blender. Return puree to soup.
Heat and serve.

Although Thai foods are typically very spicy, this soup is creamy and delicate. Don't be put off by the seemingly spicy ingredients.

Eggs & Cheese

Cheese "Sandwiches"

8 ounces (225 gr) eggplant,
   unpeeled

2½ ounces (70 gr) sharp cheese
   (kashkaval, halumi, etc)

prepared hummous (pureed
   garbanzo bean salad)

1 beaten egg

1 teaspoon soy sauce

¾ cup bread crumbs

1 teaspoon dried parsley

salt and pepper to taste

1 cup vegetable oil

❶ Cut eggplant in half across. Then cut each half lengthwise in 6 thin slices, ¼ inch (0.64 cm). (You should have 12 slices). Salt both sides of eggplant lightly with salt. Drain ½ hour. Rinse, squeeze and pat dry. Pair the slices to make 6 pairs.

❷ Cut cheese in 6 thin slices, ¼ inch (0.64 cm) in lengths to fit on the eggplant slices.

❸ Spread hummous on both sides of cheese slices. Insert 1 cheese slice into each eggplant pair and press together. (The hummous binds the cheese and eggplant).

❹ In a soup bowl, combine beaten egg and soy sauce.

❺ In another soup bowl, combine breadcrumbs, parsley, salt and pepper.

❻ Heat oil in a wok or deep pan. When hot, dip each sandwich first into egg mixture then into bread crumbs and add to hot oil. (Add 2 or 3 sandwiches at a time). With a ladle or spoon, carefully ladle hot oil over top of each sandwich. Fry until browned. Drain well on paper towels.
Serve hot or at room temperature.

Note:
To reheat: deep fry in hot oil very briefly, being careful not to let the cheese ooze from the eggplant.

These yummy eggplant "sandwiches" make a dandy appetizer or snack anytime.

Chauchouka

1 small (8 ounces \ 225 gr)
  eggplant, unpeeled, cubed
  ¼ inch (0.64 cm)

2 tablespoons oil or margarine

1 large green pepper, diced

1 medium onion, chopped

3 small tomatoes, thinly sliced in
  rounds

4 eggs, beaten

salt and pepper to taste

❶ **S**alt cubed eggplant and allow to drain about
15 minutes. Wash, drain again, squeeze out the
liquid and pat dry.

❷ **I**n an oven proof fry pan, heat oil or margarine.
Add cubed eggplant, green pepper, and onion and
saute until onion and eggplant are soft.

❸ **L**ay tomatoes on top of vegetables. Cover and
cook until soft.

❹ **A**dd beaten eggs, salt and pepper. Cover and cook
until eggs are set on bottom.

❺ **P**lace fry pan under a hot grill for several minutes
until eggs have set on top.
Serve hot or cold.

Variation:

*Instead of using beaten eggs, drop in whole eggs evenly
around the pan and cook them "sunny side up". When
cooked this way, there may be no need to use the grill
to set the eggs.*

*T*his egg dish is popular throughout the Middle East. Kiosks sell it in the morning as a quick
breakfast for people on the run. They serve it stuffed in a pita with fried potatoes and salads. It
also makes a fine luncheon meal. I vary the standard recipe by adding eggplant and serving it on
a plate, with a lettuce salad or cole slaw and rice cakes or bread. And, because it is also
delicious served cold, it is a fine choice for a buffet or snack.

Davasco Vegetable Pie

1½ pounds (680 gr) eggplant, peeled, cut in 1 inch (2.5 cm) cubes

1 teaspoon salt

1 medium onion, chopped

½ sweet green pepper, chopped

1 clove garlic, minced

1 egg, slightly beaten

2 tablespoons butter or margarine, melted

½ cup dry bread crumbs

½ teaspoon dried basil

½ teaspoon dried oregano

¼ teaspoon pepper

1 teaspoon lemon juice

½ heaping cup coarsely grated sharp cheese (cheddar, kashkaval, etc)

¼ cup finely grated Parmesan cheese

1 large tomato, thinly sliced

½ teaspoon sugar (optional)

paprika

❶ In a large pot, add eggplant cubes, salt and water to cover cubes 1 inch (2.5 cm). Bring water to a boil. Lower heat and simmer until tender, about 10 to 15 minutes.

❷ Meanwhile, in a medium pot, cook onion and green pepper covered in a small amount of water until tender, about 3 to 5 minutes. Drain and set aside.

❸ Drain eggplant cubes, pressing out as much moisture as you can. (Eggplant may begin to mash.) Transfer to a bowl or food processor. Reduce eggplant to a pulp, either with a fork or food processor. Add onion, green pepper, garlic, egg, butter or margarine, bread crumbs, basil, oregano, pepper, and lemon juice. Continue processing until well blended.

❹ In a medium bowl, mix together the two cheeses.

❺ Grease a baking pan (or use non-stick spray) approximately 10×6½×2 inches (25.5×16.5×5 cm). Spread eggplant mixture into baking pan, smoothing the top. Lay tomatoes over top. Sprinkle with sugar. Distribute cheeses evenly over all. Sprinkle with paprika.

❻ Bake in a preheated 350 F (180 C \ gas mark 4) oven for 30 minutes. Allow to set about 10 to 15 minutes before cutting.
Serve hot.

This recipe is adapted from a specialty of Davasco, a chef in Bologna, Italy. Some call it a kugel; some call it a casserole. But whatever its name, you will call it delicious. It makes a fine vegetarian meal accompanied by other vegetables or salads.

Chilaquiles

2 teaspoons butter or oil

12 fried tortilla chip snacks

4 eggs, beaten

1 cup drained Salsa Cruda with Eggplant. See page 39 for recipe.

3 ounces (85 gr) cheddar cheese, coarsely grated

½ cup water

⅓ cup finely snipped parsley

❶ **M**elt butter or oil in a non-stick fry pan. (Otherwise you may need to add more butter or oil.) Lay tortilla chips around the pan.

❷ **P**our the beaten eggs over the tortilla chips and cook until chips are coated and eggs are set on bottom.

❸ **S**pread in the Salsa Cruda, pressing it down gently into the eggs. Sprinkle in half the cheese. Pour in the water around the rim of the pan. Simmer uncovered until the water evaporates, about 10 or 15 minutes.

❹ **R**emove to a serving plate. Sprinkle first the cheese then the parsley around the edges. Serve warm.

Note:

If prepared fried tortilla chip snacks are unavailable, tear corn tortillas in 2 inch (5 cm) pieces. Fry tortilla pieces in ½ inch (1.25 cm) hot oil for almost a minute, until they are crisp and golden.

Chilaquiles is a colorful Mexican egg and cheese dish. Mexicans also call it Tortilla Skillet because it is made in a fry-pan. Serve it in wedges for brunch, lunch, or on a buffet table. Accompany this high protein dish with a salad and/or pickles.

Calzones – A Pizza Turnover

1 tablespoon olive oil

1 small onion, chopped

1 small (6 ounces \ 170 gr) eggplant, peeled, diced. See Note A.

3 small tomatoes, diced (to make 1 cup)

1 teaspoon parve chicken soup powder

dash garlic powder

dash freshly ground black pepper

4 ounces (115 gr) grated cheese (cheddar or mozzarella)

4 pieces mallawah or 7 inch (17.7 cm) rounds of pizza dough. See Note B.

❶ **I**n a pot or fry pan, heat the oil. Add onion and saute until softened.

❷ **A**dd diced eggplant, stir briefly. Add tomatoes, parve chicken soup powder, garlic powder, and black pepper. Lower heat, cover and cook until eggplant and tomatoes are soft. Uncover and reduce liquid, if any.

❸ **R**emove pan from heat. Allow to cool briefly. Stir in grated cheese.

❹ **O**n half of each of the mallawahs, leaving a free ½ inch (1.25 cm) all around, spread one fourth of the vegetables and cheese mixture. Fold the top half over the mixture, pressing the edges of dough firmly together with your fingers. Pierce top in three places with a knife edge.

❺ **L**ightly grease (or use non-stick spray) a baking pan large enough to hold calzones. Bake in a hot oven, 475 F (245 C \ gas mark 9) for 8-10 minutes, until tops are golden brown. Serve hot.

Notes:

A: If a small eggplant is not available, cut 6 ounces from a larger eggplant.

B: If using pizza dough: at step 4, paint the surface with olive oil before spreading on the vegetable and cheese mixture. Paint the top with olive oil before piercing.

*M*allawah, a Yemenite dough, is made with flour, water and butter. It is usually eaten fried with a sweet such as honey, or with a fiery red hot sauce. I like to use it as a pastry or pizza dough, as in this recipe. It is available ready made in the frozen food section of many super markets. If mallawah is unavailable, use pizza dough.

Eggplant Parmigiana

Ingredients

1 pound (455 gr) eggplant

non-stick vegetable spray or oil

1 medium onion, chopped finely

1 medium green pepper, diced

2 cloves garlic, minced

1 cup prepared spaghetti sauce

¼ teaspoon dried oregano

½ teaspoon dried basil

salt and pepper to taste

¼-½ cup water

4 ounces (115 gr) part-skim mozzarella cheese, coarsely grated

¼ cup Parmesan cheese, finely grated

Directions

❶ **S**et oven to 350 F (180 C \ gas mark 4). Peel eggplant if desired, or wash skin well. Slice eggplant crosswise into ¼ inch (0.64 cm) slices.

❷ **L**ine a large baking pan (10×15 inches \ 25.4×38 cm) pan with aluminum foil. Spray with non-stick spray, or oil lightly. Place eggplant slices on foil. Try not to overlap slices. Cover with another piece of aluminum foil and bake for 15 to 20 minutes, until slices are soft. (Microwave: Use glass utensil; cover with plastic, cook on High for 3 to 5 minutes).

❸ **W**hile eggplant is baking, prepare vegetables. In non-stick pan, or one sprayed with non-stick spray, saute onion, green pepper and garlic over moderate heat, until onion is soft. (Microwave: cook 1 minute on High).

❹ **A**dd spaghetti sauce, oregano, basil, salt and pepper. (If spaghetti sauce is very thick, add water). Let simmer for 5 minutes.

❺ **R**emove eggplant from oven. Remove top foil. Cover eggplant evenly, first with sauce, then with mozzarella cheese, then with Parmesan cheese.

❻ **R**eturn to oven, uncovered, and bake until cheese melts. This takes only a few minutes.
Serve at once. (Microwave: 2 minutes on Medium).

*M*y version of this Italian classic is still one of my favorite ways to serve eggplant. I used this recipe in my Healthy Pregnancy Menu Cookbook and it got rave reviews because much of the fat content is omitted but we keep all the rich flavor. The dish makes an excellent lunch with a side salad or vegetable, or serve it with pasta. I have included microwave directions, but I prefer the taste when baked in the oven.

Eggplant-Tomato-Cheese Wheel

For Each Wheel:

olive oil

1 slice unpeeled eggplant, cut across ½ inch (1.25 cm) from widest part

½-1 teaspoon creamy Italian dressing

dash garlic powder

1 slice tomato, cut across ½ inch (1.25 cm)

1 slice kashkaval cheese, ½ ounce (14 gr), or other yellow cheese

soybean BBQ bits

dash paprika

❶ Line a baking pan with aluminum foil. Lightly grease foil or spray with non-stick spray. (Pan should be large enough to hold all eggplant slices you will be using.)

❷ Brush a thin layer of olive oil on both sides of each eggplant slice. Place the slices on the baking pan and broil for 3-5 minutes each side, until golden brown.

❸ Spread Italian dressing on top of each slice and add dash of garlic powder.

❹ Layer first the tomato, then the cheese on each slice.

❺ Bake for about 10 minutes in preheated oven (350 F \ 180 C \ gas mark 4), until the cheese is half-melted. Remove from oven and decorate with a few BBQ bits and paprika over cheese. Serve hot.

This baked eggplant dish can be served as a nosh or as a side vegetable with egg or fish dishes. The recipe tells you how to prepare one wheel. Prepare each additional wheel in the same way. Allow one or two cheese wheels per person.

Mallawah Eggplant Pie

Dairy
Serves 4

1 mallawah

1 medium (8 ounces \ 225 gr) eggplant, peeled, cubed ¼ inch (0.64 cm)

2 eggs

2 ounces (55 gr) coarsely grated cheddar cheese

1 small tomato, diced

1 tablespoon salsa (homemade or store bought)

salt and pepper to taste

❶ Lightly oil (or use non-stick spray) a 9 inch (22.9 cm) pie plate.

❷ With a rolling pin, press out slightly thawed mallawah to fit the pie plate. (For ease in rolling out, do not remove separating plastic papers.)

❸ Remove separating plastic papers. Place mallawah in the bottom and up the sides of the pie plate.

❹ Cook eggplant cubes in one cup of salted boiling water about 5 minutes, until softened. Drain well, squeezing out excess juices with the back of a wooden spoon. (Do not mash).

❺ In a bowl, beat eggs. Mix in eggplant, cheese, tomato, salsa, salt and pepper. Pour egg mixture into mallawah. See Note.

❻ Bake at 350 F (180 C \ gas mark 4) for 30 minutes, until eggs are set and mallawah is brown and puffy. Let stand a few minutes before cutting in wedges.

Note:

The egg mixture may look skimpy when placed in the pie plate, but it will rise when baked. During baking the mallawah will slip down somewhat from the sides of the pie plate and will puff up beautifully and brown nicely.

Mallawah is a Yemenite dough made with flour, water and butter. It is usually fried and eaten with either honey or a fiery red hot sauce. In this recipe, I use it as a pastry base. It makes a delightful main meal with a green salad and a vegetable. It's a winner, too, when served as a snack, or a starter to the main meal. In many super markets, mallawah is sold frozen in packages of 10 or 12 rounds. If mallawah is not available, use filo dough or a pastry crust.

Y'eggs Mount Vesuvius

1 medium onion, chopped

1½ tablespoons olive oil

2 large ripe tomatoes, diced

2 cloves garlic, minced

⅓ cup diced sweet red pepper

1½ tablespoons tomato puree

2 teaspoons light brown sugar

½ teaspoon salt

1 teaspoon lemon juice

4 slices eggplant, each ½ inch
(1.25 cm) thick, cut from widest
part of plant, approximately
3-4 inches (7.6-10 cm) in
diameter

½ teaspoon dried oregano

1 teaspoon butter or oil

4 eggs

4 slices cheddar cheese, cut in
strips 1×2 inches (2 .5×5 cm)

❶ **P**repare tomato sauce: in a saucepan, saute onion in ½ tablespoon olive oil until golden. Add tomatoes, garlic, diced sweet red pepper, tomato puree, brown sugar, salt, lemon juice. Mix and cook over moderate heat about 15 minutes, stirring occasionally.

❷ **W**hile sauce is cooking, prepare eggplant slices: in a fry pan, preferably non-stick, add ½ tablespoon olive oil. Over moderate heat fry eggplant slices, covered, until golden. Add remaining ½ tablespoon oil, turn eggplant, cover pan and continue cooking until soft and golden. Drain on paper towels. Reserve.

❸ **A**t the end of the 15 minute cooking time for the tomato sauce, remove from heat, add oregano and mix in. Reserve.

❹ **A**dd 1 teaspoon butter or oil to the fry pan. Drop in the eggs and fry them sunny-side up. Cook until set.

❺ **T**o serve: spoon about ⅓ cup tomato sauce onto each serving plate. Top each in the following order: 1 slice eggplant, a little more tomato sauce, 1 slice cheese and 1 egg. Serve immediately, 1 to 2 Y'eggs per serving.

Note:

This recipe can be increased by using additional eggplant slices, cheese and eggs. Keep any excess tomato sauce in the refrigerator for use in another meal.

This tasty dish makes an excellent luncheon or lazy-day breakfast. I named it after Mount Vesuvius because the stacking of eggplant, sauce, cheese and egg makes a pyramid which reminds me of the volcano in southern Italy that destroyed Pompeii and Herculon.

Syrian Vegetable Omelet

Dairy
Serves 4

½ cup boiling water

1 medium onion, diced

1 heaping cup sliced cauliflower
florets

1 small to medium (6-8 ounces \
170-225 gr) eggplant, peeled,
diced

½ cup diced fresh tomatoes

1 teaspoon dried dill

¼ teaspoon cinnamon

½ cup coarsely grated sharp sheep
cheese (gilad, kashkaval)

4 eggs, beaten

salt and pepper to taste

❶ **I**n a large fry pan, preferably non-stick, add
boiling water, onion and cauliflower florets. Cover
and simmer 5 minutes.

❷ **A**dd diced eggplant. Cover and simmer another
5 minutes.

❸ **M**ix in tomatoes, dill and cinnamon. Cover and
simmer 2 to 3 minutes.

❹ **R**emove pan from flame. Stir in cheese. Press
vegetables into pan. Return to flame.

❺ **P**our beaten eggs over all. Cover over low heat
until eggs are set, about 3 to 5 minutes. Cut
serving pieces in the pan.
Serve hot or warm.

Note:

*To prevent scratching the surface of a non-stick fry
pan, use a plastic knife or spatula to cut into serving
pieces. Alternatively slide omelet onto a serving dish
before cutting.*

*This omelet shows its Syrian origins by the unusual combination of dill and cinnamon and by
its use of sheep cheese. Lower the fat content by using a non-stick fry pan. If not available, first
add a little oil, butter or non-stick spray to your regular fry pan and proceed with the recipe to
achieve the same results.*

Pizza Napoli

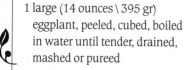

For The Crust:

1 large (14 ounces \ 395 gr)
eggplant, peeled, cubed, boiled
in water until tender, drained,
mashed or pureed

½ cup flour

2 teaspoons baking powder

1 teaspoon salt

1 tablespoon corn meal

For The Sauce:

1 tablespoon plus 1 teaspoon
olive oil

1 cup diced tomatoes, drained

3 fresh basil leaves, minced or
½ teaspoon dried basil

½ teaspoon dried oregano

dash black pepper

For The Topping:

½ small onion, sliced

½ small green pepper, sliced in
half-rings

½ heaping cup grated mozzarella
cheese

2 sliced green olives and 2 sliced
black olives (optional)

❶ Combine mashed or pureed eggplant with flour,
baking powder and salt.

❷ Lightly grease a pie pan (9 inches \ 22.9 cm). (Can
use non-stick spray.) Sprinkle bottom with corn
meal. Pour eggplant mixture into pie pan. Pat
down evenly on the bottom and up the sides. Bake
in a preheated oven 350 F (180 C \ gas mark 4) for
about 15 minutes, until crust is firm. Reserve.

❸ In a fry pan (preferably non-stick) heat
1 tablespoon oil. Add tomatoes, basil, oregano
and pepper. Saute until moisture evaporates.

❹ Spread 1 teaspoon oil over base of eggplant crust.
Spread tomato sauce over base. Place onion slices
and green pepper slices in a pattern over the
sauce. Sprinkle top with cheese. Optional:
Sprinkle olives over cheese, alternating the green
and black colors.

❺ Raise the oven to 375 F (190 C \ gas mark 5).
Bake until cheese has melted and is lightly
browned.
Cut into wedges and serve.

In Naples I was served pizza with a paper thin crust that had a delicately flavored sauce of fresh tomatoes. I have adapted the Neapolitan way of preparing pizza which produces a lovely light dish for one of the world's favorite foods.

Roll-Ups

12 slices unpeeled eggplant, cut ¼ inch (0.64 cm) across from the widest part. Each slice should be 3 to 4 inches (7.5 to 10 cm) diameter

2½ ounces (70 gr) finely grated cheese from three different types: smoked provolone (bashan), kashkaval, mozzarella

½ teaspoon parve chicken soup powder

½ teaspoon onion soup powder

½ teaspoon mushroom soup powder

⅛ teaspoon garlic powder

dash black pepper

olive oil

❶ **P**reheat oven to 475 F (245 C \ gas mark 9).

❷ **G**rease a large baking pan or spray with non-stick spray. Lay eggplant slices on pan. (Try not to overlap slices). Cover with aluminum foil and bake 10 minutes on each side. Eggplant should be soft enough to roll. If not, bake longer.

❸ **I**n a medium bowl, add cheeses, soup powders, garlic powder, black pepper, and blend.

❹ **P**lace a heaping teaspoon of cheese mixture slightly below the center of each eggplant slice and roll up, pressing down gently to seal.

❺ **R**eturn roll-ups, flap side down, to baking pan. Spread tops with a dab of olive oil and bake about 5 minutes, until golden brown and cheeses have melted. Serve hot, 2 to 3 roll-ups each person.

Note:
For ease in grating cheeses, hold all three types in your hand while grating.

Micro Tip:
Instead of baking eggplant slices at Step 2, use the microwave. On a micro-safe pan, cook eggplant slices covered on High for one minute each slice. Then proceed with recipe.

This is a unique appetizer or snack. I think it is tastier when baked in the oven to soften the eggplant, but good results can be achieved by using the microwave. See Micro Tip above. Try other combinations of cheeses for different taste treats.

Souffle I

1 medium (12 ounces \ 340 gr) eggplant, peeled, cubed ½ inch (1.25 cm)

2 tablespoons butter

2 tablespoons flour

½ teaspoon dry mustard

½ teaspoon salt

1 cup milk

2 eggs, separated

1 tablespoon bottled chili sauce or ketchup

½ cup grated Swiss cheese

bread crumbs

Note:
Separate eggs while they are cold. Keep egg whites at room temperature before beating to increase volume.

❶ Cook eggplant cubes in boiling water until tender. Drain well. Mash by hand or puree in food processor. Reserve.

❷ In a saucepan, melt butter. Add flour, mustard and salt. Blend until smooth and free of lumps. Gradually add milk while stirring with a whisk. Continue cooking and stirring until mixture has thickened. Remove pan from heat.

❸ Beat egg yolks until light and creamy. Stir beaten egg yolks into thickened mixture and return pan to heat.

❹ Add reserved eggplant cubes, chili sauce or ketchup and Swiss cheese. Stir until well-blended and cheese has melted. Remove pan from heat.

❺ Beat egg whites until stiff, not dry. Fold into eggplant mixture.

❻ Lightly grease the bottom and sides of a 6 inch (15.25 cm) souffle dish. Sprinkle a light coating of bread crumbs over greased bottom and sides. Pour eggplant mixture into souffle dish. Set in a pan of hot water. Bake at 350 F (180 C \ gas mark 4) for 35-45 minutes. (Test for doneness by giving the dish a gentle shove. It is done if the top crust moves very slightly. If it trembles, continue to cook.)
Serve immediately.

This recipe and the one following have most of the same ingredients, but the method of preparation is somewhat different. This souffle is baked using a hot water bath, contains no bread crumbs in the mixture and produces a fairly moist dish. Each souffle is so good that I can't decide which one I like best. Souffles make excellent luncheon meals and late night suppers.

Souffle II

1 medium (12 ounces \ 340 gr) eggplant, peeled, diced

2 eggs, separated

2 tablespoons flour

½ teaspoon dry mustard

½ teaspoon salt

dash white pepper

2 tablespoons butter

1 cup milk

1 tablespoon bottled chili sauce or ketchup

½ cup bread crumbs

½ cup grated Swiss cheese

❶ **B**oil diced eggplant in water until tender. Drain well. Mash by hand or puree in blender or food processor. Reserve.

❷ **B**eat egg yolks until light and creamy. Reserve.

❸ **I**n a small bowl, combine flour, mustard, salt and white pepper.

❹ **I**n a saucepan, melt butter. Add flour mixture and stir until smooth. Gradually add milk while stirring with a whisk. Continue cooking and stirring until mixture has thickened. Stir in reserved beaten egg yolks, chili sauce or ketchup.

❺ **S**tir in pureed eggplant, bread crumbs. Remove from heat. Stir in cheese until melted.

❻ **B**eat egg whites until stiff, not dry. Fold into eggplant mixture.

❼ **P**our into a 6 inch (15.25 cm) souffle dish. Bake in a preheated oven 325 F (160 C \ gas mark 3) for 30 minutes or until done. (Souffle is done when top crust barely trembles when the dish is pushed gently).
Serve immediately.

Note:

This dish can also be made with frozen eggplant. As the eggplant has already been parboiled in the freezing process, there is no need to boil it again. Simply defrost, drain and mash or puree.

This is the second souffle recipe. Because it uses bread crumbs, it produces a slightly thicker, firmer souffle than the preceding recipe. The mixture is poured into a dry dish and does not use a water bath, as in the first recipe. Both are delicious. Try each to decide which you like best.

Spanish Eggplant Casserole

1 medium (12 ounces \ 340 gr) eggplant, peeled, cubed ½ inch (1.25 cm)

1 tablespoon vinegar

2 slices Italian bread, cut 1 inch (2.5 cm) wide.

½ cup thinly sliced pitted black olives

1 cup prepared spagetti sauce

2 cups canned or frozen corn kernels, drained. If using frozen kernels, cook briefly

2 eggs, beaten

1½ cups coarsley grated cheddar cheese

❶ **B**ring a pot of water to a boil. Add eggplant cubes and vinegar. Parboil for 5 minutes, until eggplant cubes are soft. Drain well.

❷ **S**oak bread in water until soft. Squeeze dry and crumble.

❸ **I**n a large bowl, mix all ingredients together, reserving ½ cup of cheese.

❹ **P**our into a greased oven proof casserole or one sprayed with non-stick spray. Pat down evenly. Sprinkle remaining ½ cup of cheese over top.

❺ **B**ake at 350 F (180 C \ gas mark 4) for 35 to 45 minutes, until golden brown and puffy. Let stand 5 to 10 minutes to set. Spoon out to serve.

This colorful dish makes a wholesome brunch or luncheon meal for hearty eaters. It also goes well on a buffet table.

Mock Pizza Slices

1 pound (455 gr) eggplant, unpeeled, sliced ½ inch (1.25 cm)

olive oil

½ cup prepared pizza sauce

3½ ounces (100 gr) mozzarella cheese, coarsely grated

sliced black and or green olives (optional)

❶ **L**ine a large baking tray with aluminum foil.

❷ **P**lace eggplant slices on tray. Try not to overlap the slices. Brush the eggplant slices on both sides with olive oil.

❸ **C**over the eggplant slices with another piece of aluminum foil. Bake in a 350 F oven (180 C \ gas mark 4) for 30-35 minutes, until eggplant slices are soft. Remove from oven. Remove top piece of aluminum foil.

❹ **C**over each eggplant slice with pizza sauce. Sprinkle grated mozzarella cheese over the top. Optional: top cheese with slices of black and or green olives.

❺ **R**eturn tray to oven. Bake uncovered until mozzarella cheese melts, about 5 minutes. Serve hot.

Variation:

For a different taste treat, use prepared salsa and crumbled feta cheese instead of pizza sauce and mozzarella cheese.

These easy to make mock pizza slices eliminate all the flour. Kids love them as a snack. They also can be served as a side vegetable in a fish or dairy meal.

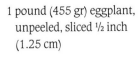

Fish Recipes

Caribbean Curried Fish

1 large onion, chopped

5 tablespoons butter or margarine

1 medium apple, unpeeled, cored, diced

¼ cup pitted, chopped dried dates

8 ounces (225 gr) eggplant, unpeeled, diced

1 cup canned pineapple pieces, drained

1½ teaspoons curry powder

½ teaspoon Tabasco sauce

1 scant cup sherry wine

3 tablespoons white flour

1½ cups milk

10 ounces (285 gr) firm fish fillets, cut in bite size pieces

salt to taste

❶ **I**n a pot, saute onion in 2 tablespoons butter or margarine for 5 minutes, until softened and slightly golden.

❷ **A**dd 1 tablespoon butter or margarine. When melted, stir in diced apple, chopped dates and diced eggplant. Stir 2-3 minutes. Add pineapple pieces, 1 teaspoon curry powder and ¼ teaspoon Tabasco sauce. Simmer a few minutes.

❸ **A**dd ½ cup sherry wine. Simmer a few minutes to reduce liquid.

❹ **I**n a small bowl, blend the flour and ⅓ cup milk. Add to the onion, fruit and eggplant mixture. Cook and stir until thickened.

❺ **I**n a separate pan, heat the remaining milk (do not boil.) and add to the thickened mixture. Simmer about 10 minutes, stirring frequently. Remove from heat. Keep warm, covered.

❻ **I**n a non-stick fry pan, saute fish in remaining 2 tablespoons butter or margarine. Stir in remaining ½ teaspoon curry powder, ¼ teaspoon Tabasco sauce and remaining scant ½ cup sherry wine. Cover. Cook about 10-12 minutes until fish is done.

❼ **C**ombine fish with reserved fruit and eggplant mixture. Serve hot over rice or other grain.

This creamy, fruit-filled fish stew, is typical of the cuisine of the Caribbean Islands. Enjoy it with cole slaw or a small lettuce salad. It makes a nice family luncheon and even a special meal for guests.

Creamy Tuna & Eggplant Mold

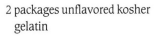

2 packages unflavored kosher gelatin

juice of ½ lemon (scant 1 tablespoon)

1 cup boiling water

1 pound (455 gr) eggplant, roasted, drained, coarsely chopped. See Note A.

1 can (6½-7 ounces \ 185-200 gr) tuna, drained and flaked. See Note B.

1 medium onion, chopped

½ cup mayonnaise

½ teaspoon prepared mustard

1 teaspoon dried dill

1 teaspoon parve chicken soup powder

dash black pepper

pinch hot chili powder (cayenne powder)

½ cup heavy cream

❶ **D**issolve gelatin and lemon juice in boiling water.

❷ **I**n a food processor or blender, add dissolved gelatin and lemon juice and all the other ingredients, except cream. Process until well blended.

❸ **W**hile processing, slowly add cream until well blended.

❹ **P**our into one oiled mold or individual oiled molds and chill until set. (Can use non-stick spray instead of oil.)

❺ **T**o serve, unmold by running a wet knife around the sides of the mold. Invert a flat serving plate over mold and turn over. The tuna mold will slip out.

Notes:

A: See page 172 for Basic Roast Eggplant recipe. Use any method.

B: One can substitute canned salmon with skin and bones removed.

*S*erving foods in a mold is all too often overlooked when preparing meals, yet it is so simple because the food processor does all the work. This creamy tuna and eggplant mold makes a colorful presentation when topped with sprigs of parsley and surrounded by salad vegetables. This recipe is ideal as a make-ahead meal because little cooking is involved. Serve it as a main meal or as a starter.

Baked Fish Creole

1 Creole Eggplant Casserole, baked. See page 129 for recipe

1 pound (455 gr) firm-flesh fish fillets (saithe, turbot, Nile perch, etc), cut in four pieces

2 teaspoons lemon juice

dash garlic powder

dash pepper

❶ **P**reheat oven to 350 F (180 C \ gas mark 4).

❷ **G**rease (or spray with non-stick spray) a baking pan or individual oven-proof gratin dishes.

❸ **S**prinkle ½ teaspoon lemon juice, garlic powder and pepper on each piece of fish.

❹ **L**ay slices of fish on the baking pan, or gratin dishes. Top each piece with equal amounts of baked Creole Eggplant Casserole.

❺ **B**ake about 20 minutes, or until fish flakes. Ready to serve.

Note:
Creole Eggplant Casserole can be made ahead and refrigerated until ready to use.

Louisiana, the home of Creole cookery, is abundant in fish of all kinds. Its cuisine includes some of the world's great fish recipes, such as Trout Amandine. This fish recipe, Louisiana style, is excellent for lunch or supper. To make a meal special, bake and serve in individual gratin dishes. Double the recipe for guests.

Fried Fish & Eggplant Stew

1 very large (1¼ to 1½ pounds \ 570-680 gr) eggplant, peeled, cut in cubes 1½ inches (3.8 cm)

1 tablespoon lemon juice

1 tablespoon butter or margarine

1 medium onion, chopped

2-3 cloves garlic, minced

14 ounces (395 gr) firm-fleshed fish fillets (Nile perch, halibut, etc.) cut in 1½ inch (3.8 cm) pieces

flour

2 tablespoons vegetable oil

½ cup finely chopped parsley

4 tablespoons bottled chili sauce

salt to taste

hot pepper to taste (cayenne powder)

1 tablespoon vegetable soup powder

1 cup boiling water

2 ounces (55 gr) kashkaval or other sharp cheese, finely grated

❶ **I**n a large pot, add eggplant cubes, lemon juice and water to barely cover the eggplants. Bring to a boil, cover and simmer for 5 minutes or more, until eggplant cubes begin to soften. Drain. Reserve.

❷ **I**n a skillet, melt butter or margarine and fry onion and garlic until transparent. Remove. Reserve.

❸ **D**ip fish in flour, shaking off excess. In the same skillet, heat vegetable oil and fry fish on both sides, 3 to 5 minutes.

❹ **I**n a large ovenproof pot or casserole, add first the eggplant cubes, then the fish, then the reserved onion and garlic, parsley, chili sauce, salt, hot pepper, vegetable soup powder and water. Cook covered 10 minutes or more, until the eggplant is soft and fish is cooked through. Spoon sauce over all.

❺ **S**prinkle top with cheese. Bake at 350 F (180 C \ gas mark 4) until cheese melts. Serve hot.

Micro Tip:

At Step 1, eggplant cubes can be quickly softened in the microwave. Cook in covered bowl with a little water on High for 3 to 5 minutes.

This fish stew is one of my favorites. Serve it in a pretty casserole, right from the oven. A salad and French or Italian bread rounds out the meal.

Fish Stew Provençale

2 large potatoes, peeled, cubed
½ inch (1.25 cm)

1 tablespoon vegetable oil or
olive oil

1 medium onion, thinly sliced

1 medium green pepper, chopped

2 cloves garlic, minced

2 cups tomato juice

¼ teaspoon salt

½ teaspoon sugar

1 teaspoon dried basil, crushed

1 medium (about 12 ounces \
340 gr) eggplant, peeled and
diced

¾ pound (340 gr) firm flesh fish
fillets (Nile perch, halibut, etc.)
cut into 2 inch (5 cm) pieces

❶ **P**arboil cubed potatoes until barely tender. Drain.
Reserve.

❷ **H**eat oil in a large pot. Add onion, green pepper
and garlic. Cook, stirring until onion is soft, not
brown.

❸ **A**dd to the pot the tomato juice, salt, sugar,
basil, eggplant and potatoes. Cover and cook
10 minutes or more until eggplant and potatoes
are softened.

❹ **P**lace fish pieces over top. Cover. Cook 5 minutes.
Then gently stir fish into vegetables and continue
cooking, covered, about 10 minutes or more, until
the fish flakes and the eggplant is tender and
potatoes are cooked through.

❺ **L**adle stew into soup bowls.
Ready to serve.

This quickly made fish stew is a meal in itself. It is reminiscent of hearty French country fare. Complement the flavors with a tart cole slaw and pickles. To make this a special dinner, serve with a chilled white wine.

Stacked Stuffed Sole

⅓ cup matzo meal

1½ teaspoons finely chopped onion

½ cup finely grated, peeled eggplant

2 tablespoons finely chopped green pepper

1 teaspoon snipped dill

1 teaspoon snipped parsley

¼ teaspoon cumin

salt and black pepper to taste

2 tablespoons melted butter or margarine

8 pieces fillet of sole (defrosted, if frozen)

1 medium onion, sliced

½ cup dry white wine

4 tablespoons finely grated mozzarella cheese

paprika

4 slices tomatoe (optional)

❶ **I**n a bowl, mix together the matzo meal, chopped onion, grated eggplant, chopped green pepper, snipped dill and parsley, cumin, salt and black pepper. Add melted butter or margarine and mix in well until it all holds together.

❷ **W**ash and pat dry sole fillets. Press ¼ of the matzo meal mixture on each of 4 pieces of fish. Top with the other 4 pieces of fish.

❸ **I**n an oiled baking pan, sprinkle the sliced onion over the pan. Place the 4 pieces of stuffed fish in the baking pan. Pour the dry white wine over the fish.

❹ **B**ake uncovered in a pre-heated oven 350 degrees F (180 C \ gas mark 4) for 10 minutes. Remove from oven. Sprinkle grated mozzarella cheese and paprika over the top of the fish. Top with tomatoe slices. Return to oven until cheese melts and tomatoes are softened, about 3-5 minutes. Serve hot.

*S*erve these stuffed fillets of sole for rave reviews. It's a time saver, too, because the stuffing can be made ahead and refrigerated until the fish is ready to be "stuffed" and baked.

Stir-Fried "Shrimp" & Vegetables With Rice Noodles

Parve
Serves 2 as a main meal;
serves 4 with another stir-
fried dish or large salad

2 tablespoons vegetable oil

2 cloves garlic, minced

½ cup thinly sliced fresh broccoli florets

½ cup thinly sliced fresh cauliflower florets

⅓ cup coarsely chopped sweet red pepper

⅓ cup thinly sliced celery

1 medium zucchini, sliced in thin rounds

½ cup thinly sliced fresh mushrooms

1⅓ cups cubed unpeeled eggplant, cut ¾ inch (1.9 cm)

9 pieces frozen kosher "shrimp" defrosted, cut in half lengthwise.

½ tablespoon parve chicken soup powder in ½ cup hot water

1 tablespoon soy sauce

1 teaspoon sugar

3-4 cups boiling water

¼ package (3½ ounces \ 100 gr) wide rice noodles, cut with scissors in approximate thirds

❶ In warmed wok or large fry pan, heat 1 tablespoon oil. Add garlic and "shrimp" and fry until "shrimp" are cooked through. Remove from wok. Reserve.

❷ To the wok, add in the following order: broccoli, cauliflower, sweet red pepper, celery, zucchini, mushrooms, eggplant and reserved "shrimp," stir-frying after each addition. Add chicken broth, soy sauce and sugar. Bring to a boil. Cover, reduce heat and continue to cook until vegetables are just tender. Remove from heat. Keep warm.

❸ In a large pot, bring 3-4 cups water to a boil. Add rice noodles. Cover and cook 3 to 5 minutes until noodles are limp. Drain well.

❹ In a fry pan, preferably non-stick, heat remaining 1 tablespoon oil. Add rice noodles. Fry and toss until noodles are well coated with oil and heated through.

❺ Transfer noodles to a large serving bowl or platter. Add stir fried "shrimp" and vegetables and mix.
Serve immediately.

This Chinese stir-fry uses mounds of fresh vegetables and a small quantity of kosher "shrimp": kosher fish which is processed to resemble real shrimp. The "shrimp" and fresh vegetables can be cut up ahead of time and kept covered in the refrigerator until ready for use. Final cooking then takes only a few minutes.

Bombay Fish

1 tablespoon oil

1 large onion, cut in half, sliced

1 large clove garlic, minced

2 teaspoons curry powder

1 pound (455 gr) eggplant, cut in half lengthwise, then cut crosswise in ¼ inch (0.64 cm) slices

1½ cups tomato juice

½ cup water

2 teaspoons parve chicken soup powder

1 pound (455 gr) firm fish fillets (turbot, Nile perch, etc.) cut in 2 inch (5 cm) wide slices

2 teaspoons lemon juice

❶ **H**eat oil in a large earthenware pot. Lightly fry onions and garlic until golden.

❷ **A**dd curry powder. Cook 2-3 minutes.

❸ **A**dd eggplant, tomato juice, water and parve chicken soup powder. Mix in. Bring liquid to a boil. Lower heat. Cover. Simmer until eggplant is softened, about 10-15 minutes.

❹ **P**lace fish slices over eggplant. Squeeze lemon juice over fish. Cover. Simmer until fish is done, about 10 minutes.

❺ **W**ith a slotted spoon, remove fish and eggplant to a serving dish. Spoon sauce over fish and eggplant.
Serve hot with rice.

This simple fish dish is based on an Indian recipe, but adapted for the western palate. It is quick to make with ingredients likely to be on hand in the kitchen.

Salmon & Eggplant Crepes

Directions are given for baking and frying crepes in a crepe griddle or an omelet pan. This recipe usually yields 15 to 19 crepes. Since the creamy combination of salmon and eggplant fills 8 to 12 crepes, you will have extra crepes to freeze for future use.

The crepe batter below uses corn meal, which increases the fiber content. It has fewer eggs than most crepe batter recipes, which helps to lower fat and cholesterol.

See the note below for preparing batter ahead and for storing and freezing crepes.

For The Crepes:

½ cup plus 3 tablespoons white flour

½ cup corn meal

pinch of salt

1¼ cup milk

2 eggs

1 tablespoon butter

For The Filling:

3 tablespoons butter

1 small onion, coarsely chopped

2 cups peeled, diced eggplant (from about 6 ounces \ 170 gr)

2 tablespoons flour

1 cup milk

1 can (7 ounces \ 200 gr) salmon, drained, bones and skin removed, flaked

2 tablespoons minced, canned red pepper strips, or pimento.

½ teaspoon hot chili pepper (or to taste)

½ teaspoon salt

yogurt or sour cream

paprika

Notes:

Batter can be refrigerated for several days. Stir well before using. Add more milk to thin, or flour to thicken, the batter to desired consistency.

To store unfilled crepes: stack with waxed paper between every crepe. Wrap securely in plastic wrap or in a plastic bag. Place between 2 paper plates or in a freezer container. Refrigerate 3-4 days or freeze up to 4 months. Thaw before separating the pancakes for use.

Crepes are fun to make and they are not at all difficult. They are, after all, just a very thin food-holding pancake. The word crepe is French, but different versions of the crepe are known around the world: the Jewish blintz, the Chinese egg roll, the Mexican enchilada, the Italian cannelloni and the Swedish plattar.

cont. ▷

Making the Crepes:

Place all crepe ingredients in a blender or food processor and process until well blended. Pour into a bowl. For each crepe, it is necessary to stir the batter as cornmeal has a tendency to sink.

A: To bake the crepes using an upside-down crepe griddle:

Pour batter into a 9 inch (22.9 cm) pie pan. Preheat griddle over medium-high heat.

Dip bottom of griddle in batter for just a moment. Lift gently and turn over. Place griddle with batter, bottom side up, over heat. Bake until batter loses wet look and edges begin to brown slightly. Turn griddle over a plate, loosen crepe with spatula and let it drop.

B: To fry crepes in a crepe or omelet pan (diameter 6-7 inch \ 15.2-17.8 cm):

Lightly oil pan (or use non-stick spray). Heat pan over medium-high heat. Raise pan over the heat as you pour in 2-3 tablespoons or ⅛ cup batter. Quickly rotate and tilt the pan to swirl the batter, so that it covers the bottom of the pan. Place the pan over the heat and fry until the bottom is golden and the top has lost its wet look. Fry only one side. Remove from pan with spatula and stack on plate. You may need to oil the pan after every 4-5 crepes.

Making the Filling:

❶ **I**n a saucepan, melt 1 tablespoon butter. Add onion and diced eggplant and saute for several minutes. Cover. Cook over low heat, stirring occasionally, until eggplant is tender, about 10 minutes. Remove vegetables and reserve.

❷ **I**n the same saucepan, melt remaining 2 tablespoons butter. Add flour and stir until blended. Over medium heat, gradually add milk, stirring constantly with a whisk. Cook until thick. Remove pan from heat.

❸ **T**o the flour mixture, add reserved onions and eggplant mixture, salmon, minced red pepper or pimento, hot chili pepper, and salt. Return pan to heat and cook until mixture is heated through. Fill the crepes by placing some filling on one half of the crepe. Fold the remaining half over the filling. Put a dollop of yogurt or sour cream on top and dust with paprika.

Serve 2-3 crepes per serving.

Mexican Fiesta

1 large (14 ounces \ 395 gr) eggplant, peeled, cubed ½ inch (1.25 cm)

2 tablespoons butter or margarine

2 tablespoons flour

1 tablespoon parve chicken soup powder and 1½ cups hot water

1 small onion, choppped

1 cup grated Swiss cheese or cheddar cheese

½ cup milk

salt and white pepper to taste

1 can (7 ounces \ 200 gr) salmon, drained, skinned and boned

2-3 small canned green chili peppers, seeded and minced

1½ cups coarsely broken corn tortilla chips

❶ **B**oil eggplant cubes in water until softened, about 5 minutes. Drain well. Reserve.

❷ **I**n a large pan, melt butter or margarine. Stir in flour until blended. Cook 1 minute, stirring constantly.

❸ **A**dd soup powder, hot water and chopped onions. Bring to a boil, stirring constantly with a whisk.

❹ **G**radually stir in cheese. Cook over low heat until cheese has melted. Gradually add milk, salt and white pepper. Cook until well blended. Remove from heat. Keep warm.

❺ **S**eparate salmon into small chunks. Add salmon, eggplant, chili peppers and 1 cup of broken tortilla chips to the cheese mixture. Stir until well mixed.

❻ **T**urn into a casserole. Decorate remaining chips around the side. Bake at 350 F (180 C \ gas mark 4) for 40-45 minutes or until heated through. If using individual casseroles, bake 30 minutes.

Note:
To prepare ahead: cook through Step 4. Cover and refrigerate. About 1 hour before serving, continue with Steps 5 and 6.

This high protein casserole can make a nice lunch with a tossed lettuce salad, or a more hearty dinner meal when served with Spanish Rice. For individual servings, bake in small, 10 ounce casseroles.

Tuna Fruity Eggplant Salad

Dairy
Serves 4 as a main meal
6-8 as an appetizer

8 ounces (225 gr) eggplant, peeled, cubed ½ inch (1.25 cm)

½ cup white wine vinegar

⅓ cup water

1 medium onion, chopped

¼ cup mayonnaise

¼ cup yogurt

2 tablespoons prepared red horseradish

⅛ teaspoons dry mustard

salt to taste

2 teaspoons lemon juice

2 teaspoons canned pineapple juice

1½ cups canned pineapple pieces, well drained

1 can (6.5 ounces \ 180 gr) tuna in water, drained, flaked

❶ In a glass or ceramic bowl, combine cubed eggplant, white wine vinegar, water and chopped onion. Cover. Refrigerate 2-4 hours. Toss occasionally.

❷ In a medium bowl, combine and blend together the mayonnaise, yogurt, prepared red horseradish, dry mustard, salt to taste, lemon juice and pineapple juice. Cover. Refrigerate.

❸ When ready to serve: drain cubed eggplant and chopped onion, reserving the marinade.

❹ In a large bowl, gently combine the pineapple pieces, flaked tuna, and drained cubed eggplant. Add the reserved mayonnaise mixture. Mix in.

To serve:

On a salad plate, place salad over shredded lettuce. Decorate side of plate with slices of tomatoes and cucumbers. Top the tuna and fruit mixture with a sprig of parsley or a slice of green pepper.

Note:

Use reserved marinade in salad dressings or other recipes.

This pink tinged salad has a tangy sweet-sour flavor that sparks the taste buds. It is an ideal warm weather lunch or light supper. Everything can be prepared ahead of time and combined at the last minute.

"Shrimp" Dinner In A Skillet

Parve
Serves 4

2 tablespoons olive oil

1 tablespoon margarine

½ pound (225 gr) eggplant, peeled, cubed ½ inch (1.25 cm)

1 medium onion, thinly sliced in half-rings

2 medium tomatoes, diced

1 cup prepared spagetti sauce

1 cup frozen peas

1 pound (455 gr) kosher "shrimp." See Note.

4 slices canned mango, cut in long thin strips

¼ cup sliced canned or fresh mushrooms

¼ cup mushroom water or water

salt and pepper to taste

❶ **I**n a skillet or deep pan, heat oil and margarine. Add eggplant cubes and onion. Saute a few minutes.

❷ **S**tir in tomatoes and cover. Cook, stirring occasionally, until eggplant cubes are soft and tender, about 10-15 minutes.

❸ **A**dd all other ingredients and cook uncovered until "shrimp" is cooked.
Serve hot with pasta or rice.

Note:
Kosher "shrimp" is kosher fish which has been processed to taste like shrimp and shaped to look like the "real thing." It is available in the super market in the frozen fish section.

This appealing meal is quick and simple, as many of the ingredients can be kept on hand to serve on those extra-busy days when you have unexpected guests. The proportions are not important, so you can add more of any of the ingredients for extra servings.

New Orleans Creole Gumbo

½ tablespoon vegetable oil

1 medium onion, chopped

½ cup chopped green pepper

½ cup chopped celery

1 large clove garlic, minced

2 tablespoons white flour

1½ cups canned crushed tomatoes

2 tablespoons tomato paste

½ pound (225 gr) eggplant, cut in
  ½ inch (1.25 cm) cubes

½ teaspoon salt

1 bay leaf

¼ teaspoon hot chili pepper
  powder

dash black pepper

½ teaspoon dried basil

¼ cup white wine

1 teaspoon brown sugar

1½ cups water

6 ounces (170 gr) frozen okra,
  defrosted, cut ½ inch (1.25 cm)

12 pieces frozen kosher "shrimp",
  defrosted, cut in half lengthwise.
  See Note

2 cups hot cooked long grain
  white rice

❶ **H**eat oil in a large heavy pot. Add chopped onion, green pepper, celery and minced garlic. Saute 2-3 minutes.

❷ **S**tir in flour and blend well.

❸ **A**dd all other ingredients except okra, "shrimp" and rice. Simmer, covered, until eggplant is slightly tender, about 10-15 minutes.

❹ **A**dd okra and "shrimp". Simmer, covered, another 10-12 minutes until okra is tender and shrimp is heated through.
Serve in soup bowls over hot cooked rice.

Note:
Kosher "shrimp" is kosher fish which has been processed to taste like shrimp and shaped to look like the "real thing."

Straight from New Orleans, in the southern-most part of the United States, comes this colorful fish meal. It is chockful of lovely vegetables. And, by using frozen kosher "make-believe" shrimp we can enjoy the authentic taste of the South.

Tuna Steaks & Eggplant With Walnut Sauce

1 pound (455 gr) tuna steaks, fresh or frozen, cut in 4 equal pieces

2 teaspoons lemon juice

dash salt

dash pepper

dash garlic powder

1 medium (14 ounces \ 395 gr) eggplant, unpeeled, sliced ½ inch (1.25 cm)

1 tablespoon olive oil

¾-1 cup walnut sauce. See page 177 for recipe.

2 tablespoons minced fresh coriander (cilantro) or parsley

❶ If tuna is frozen, defrost. Sprinkle tuna with lemon juice, salt, pepper and garlic powder. Allow to marinate 1 hour in the refrigerator.

❷ Preheat oven to 350 F (180 C \ gas mark 4).

❸ Lightly salt eggplant slices. Line a large baking pan with aluminum foil. Spray with non-stick spray or oil lightly. Place eggplant slices on foil. Try not to overlap slices. Cover with another piece of aluminum foil and bake for 15-20 minutes, until slices are soft. Remove baking pan from oven and reserve.

❹ In a large fry pan or griddle, heat olive oil. Add tuna and fry 3-5 minutes on each side, until cooked through. (If pan is not large enough for all pieces, fry in two batches.)

❺ Remove eggplant from foil. Place eggplant on an ovenproof baking pan suitable for serving. (Can overlap slices if necessary.) Lay tuna steaks over eggplant slices.

❻ Pour walnut sauce over tuna and eggplant. Return to oven for 4-5 minutes, until sauce is heated. Remove from oven and sprinkle coriander over all.
Serve hot or cold.

Tuna and eggplant make an appealing combination when enhanced with our unusual walnut sauce which is simple to make but produces rave reviews.

Tuna Stuffed Eggplant

1 medium (about
12 ounces \ 340 gr)
eggplant

2 tablespoons plus
1 teaspoon olive oil

1 small onion, finely
chopped

1 clove garlic, minced

1 can (6½ ounces \
180 gr) tuna fish in
water, drained,
shredded

1 small tomato,
chopped

¼ cup chopped pitted
green olives

1 tablespoon chopped
capers, drained

3 tablespoons
seasoned bread
crumbs

½ teaspoon dried
parsley

1 ounce (28 gr) good
melting cheese
(cheddar, mozzarella,
etc), sliced thinly

❶ **C**ut eggplant in half lengthwise. Remove pulp. (It is helpful
to use a grapefruit spoon). Leave a shell ¼-½ inch
(0.64-1.25 cm) thick. Lightly salt shells. Drain upside down.

❷ **C**hop pulp coarsely. Salt lightly and leave to drain
30 minutes. Rinse in cold water. Squeeze dry in a dish towel.

❸ **H**eat 1 tablespoon oil in a non-stick pan. (In ordinary pan,
you may need to add more oil.) Saute onion and garlic until
soft and transparent. Remove from pan. Reserve.

❹ **A**dd 1 tablespoon oil to pan. Saute chopped, drained
eggplant pulp until soft. Stir in tuna, tomato, and reserved
onions and garlic. Cook until heated through. Remove to a
bowl. Add olives, capers, bread crumbs and parsley. Mix well.

❺ **R**inse eggplant shells with cold water. Pat insides dry. Fill
with tuna stuffing, pressing down firmly as you do so.

❻ **A**rrange the filled eggplants in a lightly oiled baking pan.
With the remaining 1 teaspoon of olive oil, drizzle it equally
over each of the pieces. Add a little hot water to the baking
pan. Bake in an oven 320 F (160 C \ gas mark 3) for
20-25 minutes or until eggplant shells are soft and tops are
browned.

❼ **R**aise oven to 400 F (200 C \ gas mark 6). Arrange cheese
slices over the top of the filled eggplants. Return to oven
briefly until cheese is melted and bubbling.
Serve hot.

This recipe is well worth trying as it is less complicated than it looks. Its robust flavor enhances any meal, at lunch or dinner, and it can be served with pride to guests. I like to serve it with Ratatouille, but a large lettuce salad is equally good. The recipe can be doubled.

Poultry Recipes

Algerian Turkey Tajine

2 medium (each 12 ounces \ 340 gr) eggplant, unpeeled, sliced 1 inch (2.5 cm) thick.

1 teaspoon salt

2 tablespoons olive oil

1 pound (455 gr) skinless, boneless turkey breast, cut in ½ inch (1.25 cm) cubes

3 cloves garlic, minced

¼ teaspoon black pepper

¼ teaspoon ground ginger

½ teaspoon turmeric

¾ cup cooked or canned chick peas (garbanzo beans), drained. See Note.

2 cups boiling water

½ cup vegetable oil

1 tablespoon lemon juice

Note:

See page 173 for instructions on how to cook chick peas (garbanzo beans).

---

❶ **S**prinkle eggplant slices with 1 teaspoon salt. Drain for 30 minutes.

❷ **M**eanwhile, heat a large saucepan and add olive oil, turkey cubes, garlic, black pepper, ground ginger and turmeric. Fry at high heat, stirring frequently for about 5 minutes, until meat is golden. Add chick peas and stir again to coat with spices. Add boiling water. Cover and reduce heat. Simmer about 30 to 40 minutes until meat is tender.

❸ **W**hile meat is cooking, rinse eggplant slices under cold water and pat dry with paper towels.

❹ **I**n a wok or deep fry pan, add vegetable oil under high heat. When oil is very hot, add eggplant slices, a few at a time. Fry on both sides until golden. Remove and drain on paper towels. (Add more oil as needed). Reserve.

❺ **T**o the saucepan, add lemon juice. Taste, adjust seasoning. Add the fried eggplant slices, pressing slices down into the sauce. Cover and simmer 15 minutes, until eggplant is softened and sauce is reduced. Serve on a platter with meat in center, topped with eggplant slices and sauce.

A tajine is both the name of a type of earthenware cooking pot with a conical lid that is used extensively in North Africa, and a style of cooking which produces aromatic meat and poultry stews. A tajine can be prepared just as sucessfully in the traditional Western stew pot, as we do here. Tajines are usually served with couscous or rice.

Chicken Ratatouille In-A-Bag

1 tablespoon potato flour

1 plastic cooking bag,
   approximately 10×16 inches
   (25.4×40.6 cm)

1 pound (455 gr) boneless chicken
   breasts, cubed 1 inch (2.5 cm)

1 medium onion, sliced

1 medium zucchini, thinly sliced

⅓ cup sliced mushrooms, fresh
   or canned

1 medium green pepper, cut in
   1 inch (2.5 cm) squares

2 cups cubed unpeeled eggplant,
   cut 1 inch (2.5 cm)

1¾ cups prepared tomato sauce,
   any style

❶ **P**reheat oven to 350 F (180 C \ gas mark 4).

❷ **A**dd potato flour to cooking bag. Add chicken cubes and shake until coated with flour. Add all other ingredients and tie bag closed.

❸ **T**urn bag gently to mix flour and sauce and to coat all ingredients with sauce.

❹ **P**lace bag in a baking pan large enough to hold bag with all the ingredients. Snip with scissors 3 or 4 small slits in top of bag. Bake about 40 minutes, until chicken is tender. Remove the chicken and vegetables from the cooking bag. Transfer to a serving casserole. Serve hot.

This recipe combines the ever-popular French Ratatouille with chicken. Using special plastic cooking bags makes it easy to prepare a main meal with no messy pot to clean. For variety, substitute turkey breasts for the chicken. The recipe is chock full of vegetables and needs only pasta or rice to round out the meal.

Turkey Supreme

½ pound (225 gr) skinless, boneless turkey breast

1 teaspoon cumin

1 teaspoon dried coriander (cilantro) leaves, rubbed

½ teaspoon turmeric

½ teaspoon dried ground ginger

dash salt

dash black pepper

2 tablespoons lemon juice

2 tablespoons olive oil

1 large onion, chopped

1 large sweet red pepper, chopped

1 dried small hot red chili pepper, seeded and chopped

3 tablespoons dried coconut

2 cups cooked chick peas (garbanzo beans) or canned, drained. See Note.

1 tablespoon flour

1 medium (12 ounces \ 340 gr) eggplant, unpeeled, cubed ½ inch (1.25 cm)

1 cup chicken stock, or 1 tablespoon chicken soup powder and 1 cup water

3 tablespoons minced fresh coriander (cilantro) or parsley, for garnish

❶ **S**lice turkey breast into thin cutlets. Place between sheets of wax paper. With the side of a cleaver or mallet, pound cutlets to flatten. Cut into 1 inch (2.5 cm) square slices.

❷ **I**n small bowl, combine cumin, dried coriander leaves, turmeric, ground ginger, salt, pepper and lemon juice. Add spice mixture to turkey cubes, making sure cubes are well coated. Marinate at least ½ hour. (Can be marinated in refrigerator for up to 3 hours.)

❸ **I**n a large saucepan, heat 1 tablespoon oil. Add onion, sweet red pepper and hot red chili peppers. Saute until onions are softened. Add coconut and saute another 2 minutes. Add remaining 1 tablespoon oil. Add turkey and marinade. Mix and fry about 3-4 minutes. Add chickpeas and flour and mix well.

❹ **A**dd eggplant cubes and stock or chicken soup powder and water. Bring to a boil. Lower heat. Cover and cook at a simmer 20-30 minutes, until turkey is cooked and eggplant is tender. Stir occasionally. Transfer to a casserole. Garnish with coriander or parsley.
Ready to serve.

Note:
See page 173 for instructions on how to cook chick peas (garbanzo beans).

*T*his on-the-stove casserole is the perfect dish to serve with couscous for an authentic Middle Eastern meal. It is even better when made a day ahead to allow the flavors to blend. Instead of couscous, white or brown rice also can be used.

Easy Chicken In-A-Bag

Meat
Serves 4

4 chicken thighs

2 tablespoons flour

½ pound (225 gr) eggplant,
   peeled, cubed 1 inch (2.5 cm)

1 cup tomato sauce

1 small tomato, diced

1 teaspoon dried oregano

¼ teaspoon salt

½ teaspoon sugar

½ teaspoon dried basil

1 bay leaf

dash black pepper

1 cup chicken broth or
   1½ teaspoons chicken soup
   powder and 1 cup water

❶ **P**reheat oven to 350 F (180 C \ gas mark 4).

❷ **W**ash and dry chicken thighs.

❸ **A**dd flour to cooking bag. Add chicken thighs and shake until well coated. Add all other ingredients and tie bag closed.

❹ **T**urn bag gently to mix and coat the flour and liquid ingredients with the tomato, the spices, the chicken and the cubed eggplant.

❺ **P**lace bag in a baking pan large enough to hold bag. Snip with scissors in 3 or 4 places on top of bag. Bake about 45 minutes until chicken is tender.

❻ **O**pen cooking bag. Transfer contents to a serving bowl. Remove bay leaf.
Serve hot.

*T*his recipe uses plastic cooking bags. They are a boon in the kitchen because they are simple to use, help produce gourmet results, and they reduce the need for messy clean-up. If you are not familiar with this welcome kitchen helper, let this tasty chicken recipe introduce you to its benefits.

North African Turkey Balls

1 pound (455 gr) ground turkey

1 clove garlic, minced

½ teaspoon turmeric

½ teaspoon cumin

⅛ teaspoon black pepper

½ teaspoon ground ginger

1 tablespoon olive oil

1 large onion, cut in thinly sliced
half-rings

1 cup hot chicken broth or
1 tablespoon chicken soup
powder to 1 cup hot water

2 tablespoons tomato paste

1 very large (1½ pounds \ 680 gr)
eggplant, unpeeled, cut in
½ inch (1.25 cm) round slices

Note:
*If eggplant slices are very large, cut
them in half.*

❶ In a bowl, mix well together turkey, garlic, turmeric, cumin, black pepper and ginger. Moisten hands in cold water and shape turkey mixture into 20 walnut size balls Refrigerate balls 15 minutes to allow to firm up.

❷ Heat the olive oil in a large pot. Over high heat, add meatballs and saute until golden and browned, about 4 to 5 minutes. (Turn frequently with 2 spoons to retain meatball shape).

❸ Lower heat. Mix in onion rings. Saute briefly, then cover and cook until onions are limp.

❹ In a small bowl, mix chicken broth or chicken soup powder and water and tomato paste.

❺ Arrange eggplant slices around and over the turkey balls and onions. Pour the broth-tomato paste mixture over the eggplant. Bring the liquid to a boil. Lower heat, cover and cook until eggplant slices are softened, about 15-20 minutes.

❻ Turn eggplant slices and press them into the sauce, spooning sauce over slices. Cover and continue to cook another 20 minutes. Serve immediately.

This stew deserves gourmet status. The stews of North Africa have more liquid sauce than is typical of Western cookery. To absorb the sauce, serve over rice, couscous or mashed potatoes. Don't be afraid to use the spices indicated; the dish is flavorful, not "hot".

Ground Turkey & Vegetable Curry

Meat
Serves 4

1½ tablespoons fresh hot green chili pepper, minced

2 cloves garlic, minced

1 tablespoon minced fresh coriander (cilantro) leaves

1 small slice fresh ginger, minced

¼ teaspoon cumin

dash salt

dash white pepper

1 tablespoon vegetable oil

½ pound (225 gr) ground turkey

½ cup coconut milk. See Note.

1 onion, coarsely chopped

1 small strip lemon peel

2-3 tablespoons soy sauce

1 large (14 ounces \ 340 gr) eggplant, unpeeled, cut 1 inch (2.5 cm) chunks

2 carrots, sliced

1 cup bean sprouts

4 large leaves romaine lettuce, shredded

handful fried chinese noodles

❶ **I**n a small bowl, combine green chili pepper, garlic, coriander, ginger, cumin, salt and white pepper. With a mortar and pestle, or fork, mash seasonings.

❷ **H**eat oil in a wok or large fry pan. Add seasoning mixture and fry 1 minute. Add ground turkey. Fry until cooked through, breaking lumps to a crumble. Add coconut milk, onion, lemon peel, and soy sauce. Bring to a boil. Lower heat. Simmer 2 minutes.

❸ **A**dd eggplant chunks, carrots and bean sprouts. Cover. Cook 5 minutes until carrots and eggplant are tender. Remove lemon peel.

❹ **T**o serve: place shredded lettuce on a serving platter. Top with fried chinese noodles. Distribute turkey-vegetable mixture over noodles. Serve hot. Goes well with rice.

Note:
Canned coconut milk is available in oriental markets, but you can make your own. See page 179 for recipe.

Although India and Thailand are separated by the Bay of Bengal, they share many of the same seasonings. This recipe might be claimed by either country, and, possibly even by China. But it can be enjoyed in the West as well.

Greek Meatloaf

8-10 ounces (225-285 gr) eggplant, peeled, grated

1 pound (455 gr) ground turkey

1 egg

1 medium onion, chopped

2 tablespoons tomato paste

1-2 cloves garlic, minced

2 teaspoons lemon juice

⅛ teaspoon nutmeg

⅛ teaspoon cinnamon

⅛ teaspoon dried mint

salt and pepper to taste

❶ **P**reheat oven to 350 F (180 C \ gas mark 4).

❷ **S**alt grated eggplant. Drain while you prepare other ingredients. Then rinse in cold water over a strainer to drain away any liquid. By handfuls, squeeze dry.

❸ **I**n a large bowl, add turkey and all the remaining ingredients, except eggplant. Mix well.

❹ **M**ix the rinsed and squeezed dry eggplant into the turkey mixture. Knead the mixture (as in kneading bread) until eggplant is well mixed in and the mixture is smooth.

❺ **B**ake in a greased loaf pan 8½ × 4½ × 2½ inches (21.5 × 11.4 × 6.3 cm) for 30 minutes. Drain off accumulated fat. Allow to stand 15 minutes to firm up.
Slice and serve. Good hot or cold.

Here is a mealtime favorite, Greek style. It is pretty served on a platter topped with sliced tomatoes, sauteed sliced green peppers or a spaghetti-style sauce. It freezes well, so it can be made ahead for those last minute busy day meals. Serve it as a main meal with potatoes or spaghetti or even as a filling for sandwiches.

One Pot Chicken

2 tablespoons olive oil

2 cloves garlic, minced

½ teaspoon turmeric

½ teaspoon salt

½ teaspoon black pepper

½ teaspoon ground ginger

4 chicken thighs

1 cup chicken broth or
  1 tablespoon chicken soup
  powder and 1 cup water

2 tablespoons lemon juice

1 large onion, chopped

¼ teaspoon thyme

1 medium (8 ounces \ 225 gr)
  eggplant, peeled, cubed ½ inch
  (1.25 cm)

¼ teaspoon dried mint

1 medium green pepper, sliced

¼ teaspoon oregano

❶ **I**n a small bowl, mix oil, garlic, turmeric, salt, pepper and ground ginger. Rub mixture over chicken thighs. Place in a pot.

❷ **A**dd chicken broth or chicken soup powder and water and lemon juice. Bring to boil, lower heat, cover and simmer.

❸ **T**o the simmering broth, add in the following order, sprinkling the appropriate spice over the vegetable: onion and thyme; eggplant and mint; green pepper and oregano.

❹ **C**over and cook on stove 45 minutes to 1 hour until chicken is tender. Stir all vegetables and sauce together.
Serve hot.

Note:
To lessen fat content, refrigerate and remove fat as it cools.

---

*T*his Mediterranean specialty has Turkish and Algerian overtones which combine to produce a robust chicken dish. Serve it with rice, couscous, or pasta.

Indian Eggplant & Chicken Casserole

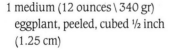

Meat
Serves 4

1 medium (12 ounces \ 340 gr)
eggplant, peeled, cubed ½ inch
(1.25 cm)

1 tablespoon vinegar

1 teaspoon dried coriander
(cilantro), rubbed

1 teaspoon turmeric

1 teaspoon cumin

1 teaspoon ground ginger

2 tablespoons olive oil

3 garlic cloves, minced

1 medium onion, chopped

1 medium green pepper, diced

3 medium tomatoes, diced

¼ cup finely snipped parsley

6-8 ounces (170-225 gr) cooked
chicken, diced

❶ **P**arboil eggplant cubes in vinegar and salted
water, covered, for about 5 minutes, until
softened. Drain well. Reserve.

❷ **I**n a small bowl, combine coriander, turmeric,
cumin and ginger. Heat olive oil in a non-stick fry
pan (otherwise you may need to add more oil).
Add spices and saute briefly.

❸ **A**dd garlic, onion, green pepper and saute until
vegetables are well coated with spices and onions
are soft.

❹ **A**dd reserved eggplant cubes, tomatoes, parsley
and chicken. Mix in and continue to saute until all
are well coated with spices.

❺ **P**our into a greased oven proof casserole or one
sprayed with non-stick spray. Pat down evenly.
Bake in a oven 350 F (180 C \ gas mark 4) for
35-40 minutes.
Serve hot. Spoon out to serve.

This zesty casserole is quickly put together and looks pretty when brought to the table straight from the oven. Try it with other cooked meats such as beef or lamb. And, by omitting the meat entirely, you have a delicious vegetarian meal or side vegetable.

Thai Noodles & Chicken With Vegetables

4 ounces (115 gr) Chinese egg noodles or spaghetti

4 Chinese dried mushrooms, soaked, thinly sliced; strain and reserve soak water

1 tablespoon vegetable oil

3 cloves garlic, chopped

8 ounces (225 gr) filleted chicken breasts, sliced across ½ inch (1.25 cm) thick

1 medium onion, sliced

1 heaping cup diced, unpeeled eggplant (about 4 ounces \ 115 gr)

1 large sweet green pepper, thinly sliced lengthwise

1 cup shredded cabbage

1 cup bean sprouts

3 tablespoons soy sauce

2 teaspoons packed brown sugar

¼ cup chopped peanuts

❶ Cook noodles according to package directions. (Cook spaghetti al dente.) Drain. Keep warm.

❷ Heat ½ tablespoon oil in a wok or large fry pan. Add garlic and fry briefly. Add chicken and fry until no longer pink. Remove. Reserve.

❸ Heat remaining ½ tablespoon oil in same wok or fry pan. Add and stir fry onion and diced eggplant 2-3 minutes, separating onion slices as you fry.

❹ Add and stir fry briefly after each addition, the green pepper, shredded cabbage, bean sprouts and mushrooms. Add soy sauce, brown sugar and 4 tablespoons reserved mushroom water. Add reserved chicken. Bring to a boil. Cover. Lower heat. Simmer 3-5 minutes until vegetables are tender but crunchy.

❺ Stir in cooked noodles or spaghetti. Heat 1 minute or until heated through. Remove to a serving platter or bowl. Sprinkle with peanuts. Serve hot.

This is a colorful stir fry dish from the magic kingdom of Thailand. It is a meal in itself, needing only a small salad to accompany it.

Chicken With Eggplant & Sage Dressing

2 tablespoons sesame seeds

1 pound (455 gr) eggplant, peeled, cubed ½ inch (1.25 cm)

1 large onion, quartered, sliced

2 tablespoons bread crumbs

2 teaspoons chicken soup powder

¼ teaspoon celery seed

2 fresh sage leaves, minced, or ¼ teaspoon dried sage

dash pepper

1 egg, beaten

2 chicken breasts, cut in half, boned

paprika

❶ **L**ightly toast sesame seeds. Reserve.

❷ **B**oil eggplant cubes and onion slices in water until tender. Drain.

❸ **I**n a bowl, combine eggplant, onion, bread crumbs, chicken soup powder, celery seed, sage, pepper, reserved sesame seeds, and beaten egg.

❹ **T**ransfer mixture to a lightly greased baking dish (or use non-stick spray).

❺ **L**ay chicken breasts over dressing. Dust with paprika.

❻ **B**ake at 350 F (180 C \ gas mark 4) for 20-30 minutes, until chicken is cooked through. Serve hot.

I've given a new twist to traditional sage dressing by topping it with chicken breasts, instead of using it to stuff a chicken or small turkey. For the calorie-conscious, skin the chicken to make the dish virtually fat-free. You might also enjoy the dressing, sans chicken, as a side vegetable.

Mediterranean Turkey & Eggplant

1 pound (455 gr) skinless,
  boneless turkey breast, cut
  1½ inches (3.75 cm) square

2 tablespoons lemon juice

3 cloves garlic, minced

¼ teaspoon white pepper

2 tablespoons olive oil

1 medium onion, sliced

2 cups unpeeled eggplant, cut in
  1 inch (2.5 cm) pieces

½ cup sliced carrots

½ cup sliced celery

½ cup tomato paste

½ cup water

½ cup white wine

½ teaspoon dried oregano, rubbed

½ teaspoon dried basil, rubbed

1 bay leaf

4 canned artichoke hearts, each
  cut in quarters

½ cup coarsely snipped fresh
  coriander (cilantro) leaves

❶ **M**arinate turkey pieces in lemon juice, garlic and pepper about 30 minutes. Turn pieces to coat well with the marinade.

❷ **I**n a large pot, on high heat, add 1 tablespoon olive oil. Add turkey pieces and saute until all pieces have turned white. Remove from pan. Reserve.

❸ **L**ower heat. Add remaining 1 tablespoon olive oil. Add sliced onions and eggplant pieces. Stir until onions begin to wilt.

❹ **S**tir in reserved turkey pieces and all other ingredients except artichoke hearts and coriander. Cover. Cook on medium heat about 40 minutes.

❺ **S**tir in artichoke hearts and coriander. Cook several more minutes until artichokes are warmed through. Remove bay leaf.
Ready to serve.

This turkey stew is chock full of vegetables found in abundance in countries bordering on the Mediterranean Sea. Serve it with Italian bread, potatoes, or a whole grain. Chicken breast can be substituted for the turkey.

Oriental Turkey Balls & Eggplant

½ pound (225 gr) ground turkey

½ tablespoon olive oil

1 pound (455 gr) eggplant, peeled, cubed ½ inch (1.25 cm)

2 large onions, quartered, sliced

1 small slice ginger, peeled, minced

¼ teaspoon finely crushed garlic

2 tablespoons soy sauce

¼ cup white wine

2 tablespoons tomato paste mixed in ¾ cup water

❶ **K**nead turkey until paste-like. With wet hands, shape into 16 walnut size balls. Place on wax paper. Cover and refrigerate at least 30 minutes to firm up. (If making ahead, turkey balls can be kept in the refrigerator for several hours if necessary.)

❷ **I**n a fry pan (preferably non-stick), heat olive oil. Brown turkey balls on all sides.

❸ **A**dd all other ingredients. Bring to a boil. Cover. Reduce heat and cook about 5 minutes.

❹ **U**ncover. Raise heat. Cook, stirring often, until most of the sauce has evaporated and thickened somewhat and turkey and eggplant are cooked through.
Serve hot.

This is a stew-like dish with flavorings from the Far East. Because it uses ground turkey and only one-half tablespoon oil, it qualifies as a low-calorie meal. It goes well with plain or stir-fried rice.

Doro Wot (A Chicken Stew)

1 chicken (2½ to 3 pounds \
   1130-1360 gr) skinned, cut into
   8 pieces

2 tablespoons lemon juice

2 teaspoons salt

¼-½ cup butter flavored vegetable
   margarine

2 cups finely chopped onions

1 tablespoon finely chopped
   cloves garlic

1 teaspoon minced ginger root

¼ teaspoon mashed fenugreek
   seeds

¼ teaspoon ground cardamon

2-3 teaspoons berbere paste.
   See page 178 for the recipe

2 tablespoons sweet paprika

¼ cup dry red wine

¾ cup water

1 medium (10-12 ounces \
   285-340 gr) eggplant, cubed
   1 inch (2.50 cm)

4 hard cooked eggs, shelled

¼ teaspoon black pepper

❶ **W**ash and dry chicken pieces with a paper towel. Rub the pieces with lemon juice and salt. Set aside for 30 minutes.

❷ **I**n a very large pot or heavy casserole, melt the margarine over medium heat. Add the onions. Saute until golden.

❸ **L**ower the heat. Add the garlic, ginger root, fenugreek, and cardamon, stirring after each addition. Add the berbere paste and paprika. Stir another 2-3 minutes.

❹ **A**dd the wine and water. Bring to a boil over high heat. Cook uncovered until the liquid has become the consistency of heavy cream, about 5 minutes. Lower heat to a simmer.

❺ **M**ix in eggplant cubes. With a fork, prick each piece of chicken and each egg all over. Add to the simmering sauce, stirring well to ensure the chicken and eggs are well coated with sauce.

❻ **C**over tightly. Simmer about 30 minutes until the chicken and eggplant are tender. Stir in the black pepper. Taste for seasoning.
Serve hot in a deep cassserole or bowl, accompanied by bread, pita or rice.

This recipe is a good introduction to Ethiopian cookery, which makes use of many spices. Ethopian stews, called "wot" or "wat" (pronounced whot), also add a fiery spice mixture called berbere. Traditionally, Ethiopians use injera, their national bread, to sop up the flavorful sauces, but you can substitute rice, pita, or any other bread.

Beef Recipes

Beef Patties With Spaghetti

For the Patties:

½ pound (225 gr) ground beef

1 tablespoon olive oil

1 small onion, sliced

8 ounces (225 gr) eggplant, unpeeled, cubed ½ inch (1.25 cm)

½ heaping cup sliced fresh mushrooms

3 medium-large tomatoes, chopped, drained

2 tablespoons coarsely chopped fresh basil or ½ teaspoon dried basil

½ teaspoon dried oregano

½ teaspoon salt

½ teaspoon minced garlic

For the Pasta:

½ pound (225 gr) spaghetti

1 tablespoon olive oil

1 teaspoon minced garlic

freshly ground black pepper (to taste)

❶ For the patties: knead ground beef until paste-like. Shape into 10-12 flat patties, about 1½-2 inches across (3.8-5 cm). Heat a heavy fry pan (preferably non-stick). Fry patties on both sides until cooked. Remove. Drain fat on paper towels. Keep warm.

❷ For the sauce: in the same fry pan, add 1 tablespoon olive oil, scraping remaining meat drippings with the oil. Add in the following order, sauteeing briefly after each addition: onions, eggplant, mushrooms, and tomatoes. Add basil, oregano, salt and garlic. Cover and cook until eggplant is softened. Reserve. Keep hot.

❸ For the pasta: cook spaghetti al dente. Drain well. To the hot spaghetti add olive oil, garlic and lots of black pepper. Toss until spaghetti is well coated with oil and spices. Keep warm.

❹ To Serve: add the reserved cooked beef patties to the sauce-eggplant mixture. Heat briefly. Transfer beef patties and sauce-eggplant mixture to a serving dish. Transfer spaghetti to a different platter or bowl. Serve both dishes and let each person take his own portion of spaghetti, beef patties and sauce-eggplant mixture. Alternatively, for a one-dish meal: in a large bowl or casserole, mix the beef patties and sauce-eggplant mixture with the spaghetti and serve.

This dish is a variation of the old standby, meatballs and spaghetti, but with a difference. The highly-flavored spaghetti is served separately from the beef patties and sauce. Round out the meal with a large salad or cooked vegetables.

Hobo Stew

1 small onion, chopped

1-2 tablespoons margarine

1 medium (14 ounces \ 395 gr) eggplant, peeled, cubed ½ inch (1.25 cm)

1 small potato, peeled, diced

1 cup frozen corn

4-5 hot dogs, sliced ½ inch (1.25 cm)

1 cup tomato juice

½ teaspoon dry mustard

1 teaspoon brown sugar

salt and pepper to taste

❶ **S**aute onion in 1 tablespoon margarine until softened.

❷ **A**dd eggplant cubes and diced potato. Saute briefly. Cover and cook until vegetables are slightly softened. Stir occasionally to prevent burning. (If necessary, add another tablespoon of margarine).

❸ **A**dd all other ingredients. Cover and cook 15-20 minutes, until potato dices are soft. Serve hot.

*B*ig and little hobos will love this hearty stew made with their favorite hot dogs. It is quickly put together with ingredients usually at hand. Serve it with crackers and a crisp salad for lunch or an evening supper.

Chinese Stuffed Eggplant

2 medium (each 10-12 ounces \ 280-340 gr) eggplants, each about 8 inches (20 cm) long. When measuring, ignore stalk.

For The Filling:

½ pound (225 gr) ground beef

1 tablespoon soy sauce

1 tablespoon dry sherry or brandy

1 green onion, whites sliced, green tops cut ¼ inch (0.64 cm)

1 thin slice ginger root, minced

½ teaspoon minced garlic

salt to taste

½ teaspoon sugar

For The Sauce:

⅔ cup water

1 teaspoon soy sauce

1 teaspoon chicken soup powder

2 teaspoons cornstarch

In this oriental recipe the eggplant is hollowed out from the center, stuffed with ground beef and steamed. You can also use other ground meats, such as turkey or chicken with the same excellent results. It is quicker to make than it appears, and because it has no added oil, it is low in calories.

cont. ▷

Meat
Serves 2-3 as a Main meal
Serves 4-6 as part of a Chinese meal

❶ **W**ash the eggplants. Leave whole with stalk. Cut a 1½ inch (3.75 cm) slice from each end of the eggplants. (At the stalk end, measure from where the stalk meets the skin.) Reserve end slices.

❷ **W**ith an apple or zucchini corer, or sharp knife, hollow out a 1 inch (2.5 cm) diameter opening from the center of the eggplants. Discard hollowed out pulp.

❸ **F**or the filling: In a medium bowl, add the filling ingredients. Mix well by hand, squeezing until meat has a paste-like texture.

❹ **S**tuff filling in hollowed out eggplant. Replace end slices, fastening them with 3 or 4 toothpicks. Reserve any extra filling.

❺ **P**lace eggplants on a heat proof dish. Steam until soft, about 20-30 minutes.

❻ **M**eanwhile, make the sauce, using remaining filling: Form the remaining filling into 1 inch (2.5 cm) round, flat "meatballs." (They should look like coins.) Fry on both sides until cooked through.

❼ **T**o the "meatballs" add ⅓ cup water, soy sauce and chicken soup powder and bring to a boil. Cook 2-3 minutes until soup powder is dissolved. Remove pan from heat. Reserve.

❽ **R**emove toothpicks and cut stalk from steamed eggplants. Discard cooked green stalk. Cut steamed eggplant crosswise in 1½ inch (3.75 cm) slices. Place the slices, (including end pieces) on a serving platter.

❾ **I**n a small bowl, combine the remaining ⅓ cup water and cornstarch.

❿ **R**eturn reserved "meatball" and sauce ingredients to heat. Bring to a boil. Add water and cornstarch mixture to the boiling sauce ingredients, stirring continuously until sauce thickens and is clear. Pour sauce and meatballs over eggplants.
Serve hot.

Indonesian Beef & Green Bean Stew

1 pound (455 gr) ground beef

2 tablespoons vegetable oil

2 cloves garlic, minced

2 teaspoons ginger root or
½ teaspoon ground ginger

1-2 fresh green chili peppers, diced

1 teaspoon dried coriander
(cilantro) leaves

4 whole green onions, whites
sliced, green tops cut ¼ inch
(0.64 cm.)

1 cup coconut milk (fresh or
canned). See Note.

1 medium (12 ounces \ 340 gr.)
eggplant, unpeeled, cubed
1 inch (2.5 cm.)

4 ounces (115 gr.) fresh or frozen
whole green beans

1 teaspoon salt

1 teaspoon sugar

❶ **C**ook beef in a fry pan, breaking up lumps until beef is crumbled and cooked through. Drain off fat. Reserve beef.

❷ **I**n a large 3-4 quart pot, heat oil. Stir in garlic, ginger root, chili pepper, coriander leaves, the white of the green onion, and fry for about 3 minutes until lightly brown.

❸ **A**dd the coconut milk. Reduce heat to medium. Stirring continuously, slowly bring the milk to a boil.

❹ **S**tir in the eggplant cubes, green beans, salt and sugar. Cover and cook 10-12 minutes until eggplant is just tender, gently stirring occasionally. (The coconut milk should continue to bubble.) Stir in reserved beef and cook briefly until heated through.

❺ **R**emove to a serving dish. Sprinkle green onion tops over beef and vegetables.
Ready to serve.

Note:

Canned coconut milk can be found in Indian markets and health food stores or you can make your own. For instructions on how to make coconut milk, see page 179.

*T*his lovely stew, steeped in coconut milk, is refreshingly different from typical western stews which have a tomato or beef base. The coconut milk imparts a delicate flavor, often found in Indonesian cookery. By eliminating the meat, you can serve it as a vegetarian meal or a side vegetable. It is perfect served over rice to soak up the delicious sauce.

Italian Beef Stew

¼ cup dry red wine

⅓ cup diced carrot

½ medium onion, minced

¼ teaspoon dried rosemary, crushed

⅛ teaspoon ground cloves

1½ pounds (680 gr) stew beef, cut in 1 inch (2.5 cm) cubes

2 tablespoons olive oil

pinch ground hot red pepper (cayenne pepper)

1 cup diced canned tomatoes

½ tablespoon minced garlic

2 cups cubed peeled potatoes, cut 1 inch (2.5 cm)

2 cups cubed unpeeled eggplant, cut 1 inch (2.5 cm)

❶ **I**n a large glass or ceramic bowl, combine the red wine, carrot, onion, rosemary and cloves. Add the beef. Marinate 3-4 hours or overnight, covered in the refrigerator. Turn occasionally.

❷ **D**rain the meat. Reserve the marinade. In a large pot, add the oil. When oil is hot, add the meat, and the hot red pepper and brown on all sides.

❸ **A**dd the marinade, bring to a boil and cook for about 3 minutes.

❹ **R**educe heat. Add tomatoes, cover and cook at a simmer for an hour or more, until meat is tender.

❺ **A**dd garlic, potatoes and eggplant, pressing them down into the sauce. Cover and cook another 15 to 20 minutes until potatoes and eggplant are soft, but not overdone.
Serve hot.

Note:

To prevent darkening: keep prepared potatoes in cold water in refrigerator until ready to use. Prepare eggplant just before adding to the meat in step 5.

---

*T*his stew can make a meal by itself, but is even better served with a salad or a vegetable, such as broccoli. It is delicious and is worth the extra effort of waiting for the beef to marinate. Although it is based on a peasant-style Italian dish, it is worthy enough to be served to guests.

Marinated Beef Liver

7 ounces (200 gr) beef liver.
  See Note

½ cup red wine

dash garlic powder

dash black pepper

½ medium green pepper

½ medium-large onion

1 large clove garlic, minced

1 tablespoon vegetable oil

1 medium can eggplants in
  tomato sauce

salt and pepper to taste

❶ Slice beef liver in ½ inch (1.25 cm) strips.

❷ In a glass or ceramic bowl, marinate beef liver strips in a mixture of red wine, garlic powder and black pepper, covered, for several hours in the refrigerator.

❸ Cut the green pepper half in thirds crosswise. Cut each third thinly lengthwise. Cut onion thinly lengthwise.

❹ In a non-stick fry pan, heat oil. Add green pepper, onion and garlic. Saute 3 minutes.

❺ Drain beef liver strips. Add to fry pan. Saute 4-5 minutes until fully cooked.

❻ Stir in can of eggplants in tomato sauce. Heat, stirring until hot. Add salt and pepper to taste. Serve hot over rice or noodles.

Note:
To kosher liver before proceding with the recipe: salt and broil on both sides until it changes color and a slight crust is formed.

If you marinate the beef liver early in the day, the final cooking will take only a few minutes because the use of a can of prepared eggplants in tomato sauce makes this dish a "snap". The recipe can be doubled.

Moussaka

Meat
Serves 4

For the Eggplant:

1½ pounds (680 gr) eggplant, unpeeled, cut crosswise in ½ inch (1.25 cm) slices

For the Sauce:

1 pound (455 gr) ground beef or ground lamb

2 cloves garlic, minced

1 medium onion, chopped

¼ cup chopped fresh mushrooms

1 tablespoon chopped fresh parsley

¼ teaspoon nutmeg

2 tablespoons tomato paste

¼ cup dry red wine

¼ teaspoon sugar

1 teaspoon chicken soup powder

dash pepper

1-2 tablespoons olive oil

For the Topping:

1 egg

1 tablespoon potato flour

½ cup mayonnaise

1-2 tablespoons water

❶ **S**alt tops of eggplant slices and allow to drain while preparing the sauce.

❷ **F**or the sauce: In a fry pan, preferably non-stick, add ground meat and cook, breaking up meat. As fat is released from meat, add garlic and onion and continue to break up meat until crumbled. Drain off fat and discard.

❸ **R**eturn meat, garlic and onions to fry pan. Add all the other sauce ingredients except olive oil. Simmer uncovered about 10 minutes. Remove pan from heat and set aside.

❹ **F**or the eggplant: Rinse eggplant slices in cold water. With paper towels, pat dry and squeeze out excess moisture.

❺ **I**n another fry pan, preferably non-stick, add 1 to 2 tablespoons oil to cover bottom of pan. Heat oil, add eggplant slices and fry on both sides until golden brown. Fry in batches until all slices are fried. (Add more oil if necessary.) Drain on paper towels.

❻ **H**eat oven to 350 F (180 C \ gas mark 4). Grease a baking pan 10×6×2 inches (25.4×15.2×5 cm) or spray with non-stick spray. Layer the baking pan with slices of fried eggplant. Spread a layer of meat mixture on the slices and continue layering, ending with eggplant slices.

❼ **F**or the topping: In a medium bowl, using a wire whisk, beat the egg. Blend in remaining topping ingredients and whisk to a creamy sauce. Spoon or pour over eggplant slices and bake until top is lightly brown, about 35 minutes.
Serve hot.

This classic Greek dish was originally borrowed from the Turks whose Ottoman Empire ruled Greece from 1400 CE until the last century. There are many variations of moussaka but the two most important ingredients are eggplant and ground lamb or beef. Toppings used also vary widely. Our topping uses mayonnaise in a creamy sauce.

Potted Liver & Eggplant

Meat
Serves 4

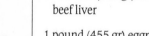

12 ounces (340 gr) thinly sliced
   beef liver

1 pound (455 gr) eggplant

2 large onions, sliced

1 clove garlic, minced

1 tablespoon cider vinegar

2 cups tomato juice

1 tablespoon vegetable oil

salt and pepper to taste

❶ **W**ash liver and pat dry. Salt lightly. Broil on a grid or rack on both sides 3-5 minutes each side, until a light crust is formed. Remove from broiler. Cut into ¾ inch (1.9 cm) cubes.

❷ **P**eel eggplant. Cut into ¾ inch (1.9) cubes.

❸ **P**ut all ingredients in an large earthenware or enamel pot. Cook covered, on low flame until eggplant is tender and sauce has reduced to about half and has thickened, about 45 minutes. Stir occasionally.
Serve hot.

This recipe is typical of traditional country cooking in Cyprus, where no one leaves the table hungry. Even if liver is not your favorite, this dish is worth a try. Serve it with mashed potatoes or crusty bread.

Stuffed Eggplant With Beef

2 tablespoons pine nuts

8 ounces (225 gr) ground beef

2 medium (each 12 ounces \ 340 gr) eggplants, unpeeled

1 tablespoon vinegar

2 tablespoons olive oil

1 medium onion, chopped

dash black pepper

dash garlic powder

¼ cup bottled chili sauce

1 cup cooked rice

1 beaten egg

1 large tomato, cut in half, sliced

❶ **I**n a fry pan, dry roast pine nuts until just golden. Remove from pan. Reserve.

❷ **A**dd ground beef, breaking up large pieces until crumbled and beef is cooked through. Drain off fat. Remove beef from pan and reserve. Wipe pan.

❸ **W**ash eggplants. Remove stalks and sepals. Cut in half lengthwise. Carefully remove pulp, leaving ½ inch (1.25 cm) thick pulp around the skin. (I find a serrated grapefruit spoon helpful in removing the pulp.) Reserve the pulp.

❹ **T**o a pot of water, add shells and vinegar. Bring to a boil and parboil eggplant shells until softened. Remove and drain well.

❺ **M**eanwhile, dice reserved pulp. In a non-stick pan, heat olive oil. (If not using a non-stick pan, you may need to add more oil.) Add onion and diced eggplant pulp and saute until eggplant is softened.

❻ **I**n a large bowl, mix together the onion and eggplant mixture, the reserved ground beef, pine nuts, pepper, garlic powder, chili sauce, rice and egg. Stuff the mixture into each half of eggplant shells. Lay 2 to 3 tomato half-slices over top.

❼ **I**n a greased baking pan, large enough to hold the eggplants side by side, lay eggplants filling side up. Bake at 350 F (180 C \ gas mark 4) for 30 to 45 minutes. Serve hot.

*T*his recipe uses the eggplant half-shells for stuffing. Parboiling the shells and cooking most ingredients prior to stuffing reduces baking time. It can be prepared ahead and reheated in an oven or microwave. Serve it as a main meal with a side salad or vegetable, or in thick slices as an appetizer.

Tunisian Stuffed Eggplant

For the Eggplant

2 medium (each 12 ounces \
   340 gr) eggplants, unpeeled, cut
   across, in 1 inch (2.5 cm) slices

salt

For the Stuffing:

8 ounces (225 gr) ground beef

3 tablespoons finely snipped
   parsley

2 cloves garlic, minced

¼ teaspoon black pepper

1 egg

For Frying:

½ cup vegetable oil

flour

1 egg, beaten

For the Sauce:

2 tablespoons oil (from the frying
   ingredients)

2 cloves garlic, minced

½ teaspoon paprika

⅛ teaspoon hot red pepper
   (cayenne pepper)

½ teaspoon cumin

1 tablespoon beef soup powder

2 cups hot water

❶ Make a deep cut half-way through the peel of each slice of eggplant. Sprinkle salt in the cut and on the top and bottom of each slice. Set aside to drain for 30 minutes. Rinse under running water and pat dry.

❷ In a bowl, mix together the stuffing ingredients until very smooth.

❸ Place ½ tablespoon stuffing into each cut of the eggplant. Spread any extra stuffing over one side of the flat surface of each slice, pressing hard to make it stick.

❹ Heat ½ cup oil in a large fry pan. Dip stuffed eggplant slices first in flour, then in beaten egg. Place in hot oil meat side down. Fry until golden on both sides. Fry in batches until all eggplant slices have been fried. Drain on paper towels.

❺ Take 2 tablespoons of oil from the frying oil. (If insufficient oil is left, use fresh oil). Add oil to a large saucepan and heat. Add the garlic, paprika, hot red pepper, and cumin. Fry gently for 2-3 minutes.Add the beef soup powder and water and bring to a boil.

❻ Arrange stuffed eggplant slices in the saucepan. Lower heat, cover and simmer 30 minutes. Serve hot with the sauce. Good with rice or other grains.

Note:

To prepare ahead: prepare eggplant as indicated in steps 1,2,3 and 4. Refrigerate covered until ready to continue. Then, about 45 minutes before serving, continue recipe at Step 5.

This is a different way to stuff eggplants. Here the stuffing is inserted into the sides of thick slices of eggplant. I like to use the white skin eggplants when available, but the purple ones are just as satisfactory. This Algerian-style tajine produces sufficient sauce to spoon over hot grains of rice, couscous or other grain.

Spicy Beefy Chili

1 pound (455 gr) ground beef

1 tablespoon plus 1 teaspoon olive oil

2 cups cubed unpeeled eggplant, cut ½ inch (1.25 cm)

1 clove garlic, minced

1 medium onion, chopped

1 medium zucchini, cubed ½ inch (1.25 cm)

1 green pepper, cut ½ inch (1.25 cm)

1 fresh hot green chili pepper, seeded, chopped

½ tablespoon beef soup powder

1 cup snipped fresh parsley

1 bay leaf

¼ teaspoons cayenne pepper, to taste

salt and pepper to taste

½ cup hot water

2 cups cooked kidney beans, or 1 can kidney beans, drained. See Note.

❶ In a large heavy pot, brown beef on moderate heat, breaking up large pieces, until beef is cooked and crumbled. Remove from pot, drain off the fat. Reserve.

❷ Add 1 tablespoon oil and eggplant cubes to pot. Saute lightly about 1 minute. Lower heat, cover and cook until softened, about 3-5 minutes, stirring occasionally. Remove eggplant cubes from pot and reserve.

❸ Over moderate heat, add remaining 1 teaspoon oil, garlic and onions and saute until softened and slightly golden.

❹ Add the reserved beef, the reserved eggplant and all other ingredients. Simmer covered about 1 hour. (Add more hot water if mixture becomes too thick.) Remove bay leaf.
Ready to serve.

Note:
To cook beans: sort and wash 1 cup of dry beans. Soak overnight in 3 cups of water, ½ teaspoon salt. Drain. Add beans to a large pot with 3 cups of fresh water, ½ teaspoon salt and 1 teaspoon oil. Simmer beans two hours, or until tender.

Suggestion:
Serve with macaroni or rice to extend this recipe to serve 8.

Native to Mexico, chili migrated north and is now loved in the United States, particularly in the south west, where contests are frequently held to determine the best chili recipe. Serve our chili with a crispy salad to cool and complement this protein-packed pungent dish.

Salami & Tomatoes
With Braised Eggplant

4 ounces (115 gr) salami slices, cut in thin strips, 1 inch (2.5 cm) long

1 medium (12 ounces \ 340 gr) eggplant, peeled, cubed 1 inch (2.5 cm)

½ teaspoon minced garlic

2 large tomatoes, coarsely chopped

salt to taste (optional)

black pepper to taste

❶ **H**eat a fry pan (preferably non-stick), add salami and fry on both sides until browned. Do not pour off any accumulated fat.

❷ **A**dd eggplant cubes, frying briefly to coat with the accumulated fat. Stir in garlic. Cover and cook under moderate heat 5 minutes, or until eggplant begins to soften. Stir once or twice.

❸ **G**ently stir in tomatoes. Cover and cook another 5 minutes or so, until eggplant is tender. Season with salt and pepper and serve.

This recipe is very easy to prepare. It has few ingredients, takes only a few minutes to cook, and is ideal for a hurry-up lunch or dinner. Serve it with fried potatoes and a salad.

Ethiopian Beef & Peppers

1 pound (455 gr) eggplant, thinly cut in julienne slices about 1½ inches (3.75) long

4 green chilis, seeded, minced

2 teaspoons fresh ginger, peeled, minced

4 cloves garlic, minced

¼ teaspoon ground cardamon

¼ teaspoon turmeric

¼ teaspoon ground cinnamon

¼ teaspoon ground cloves

½ cup dry red wine

1 pound (455 gr) steak, thinly sliced about 1½ inches (3.75 cm) long

3 tablespoons oil

2 cups chopped onions

1 green pepper, thinly sliced about 1½ inches (3.75 cm) long

¼ teaspoon black pepper

❶ **S**alt the julienned eggplant. Drain 15 minutes. Pat dry with paper towels. Reserve.

❷ **I**n a food processor or blender, puree the chilies, ginger, garlic, cardamon, turmeric, cinnamon, cloves and red wine until finely ground and paste-like. Reserve.

❸ **I**n a large heavy pot, brown the beef strips in 2 tablespoons of hot oil. Remove beef from pot. Reserve.

❹ **A**dd 1 tablespoon oil to pot. Saute the onions until softened. Do not brown. Add eggplant. Saute until slightly softened. Add the chilli puree. Bring to a boil, stirring constantly.

❺ **A**dd the reserved beef. Mix until beef strips and eggplant are coated with the sauce. Stir in black pepper. Reduce the heat. Cover. Simmer for 10 minutes.

❻ **S**tir in green pepper strips. Cover. Simmer another 10 minutes until the beef strips are done, the eggplant is soft, and the green pepper is still crisp. Serve hot over rice or use pita bread to sop up the sauce.

This dish adds an authentic spicy Ethiopian flavor to our familiar beef, peppers and eggplant. To add more 'bite', serve it with berbere paste on the side, allowing diners to adjust the taste to their liking. See page 178 for the recipe for berbere paste.

Vegetable Recipes

Baked Eggplant "Fingers"

Parve
Serves 4

1 pound (455 gr) eggplant, either two small or one large

salt

½ cup corn meal

dash garlic powder

¼ teaspoon dried dill

¼ teaspoon dried oregano

¼ teaspoon dried parsley

¼ teaspoon paprika

dash pepper

salt to taste

vegetable oil

⅓-½ cup vegetable oil

❶ **P**reheat oven to 425 F (220 C \ gas mark 7).

❷ **C**ut unpeeled eggplant lengthwise into "fingers" approximately 1 inch wide×1 inch thick×3 inches long (2.5 cm wide×2.5 cm thick×7.5 cm long). Salt lightly.

❸ **I**n a medium bowl, combine well corn meal, garlic powder, dill, oregano, parsley, paprika, pepper and salt.

❹ **S**pread a thin layer of vegetable oil over the bottom of a baking pan large enough to hold all the eggplant "fingers" in one layer.

❺ **A**dd ⅓ cup vegetable oil to a shallow dish. (Add more oil as needed.) Dip each "finger" in oil on all sides, then coat with seasoned corn meal. Lay "fingers" on baking pan.

❻ **B**ake 10 minutes, turn fingers and bake another 10 minutes or more, until eggplant is soft. Serve hot.

These corn meal eggplant fritters make a tasty treat. They are baked, not fried, and go well with any meal.

Celery & Eggplant Pancakes ("Latkes")

2 full ribs celery

1 cup celery leaves

1 small onion

¼ cup finely snipped fresh parsley

1 very large (over 1 pound \ 455-500 gr) eggplant, peeled, finely chopped

1 egg

½-1 teaspoon salt

garlic powder, to taste

½ cup plus 2 tablespoons flour

½ teaspoon baking powder

¼ teaspoon chili powder or cayenne powder

oil for shallow frying

❶ Chop fine by hand, or food processor, celery, celery leaves, onion, and parsley.

❷ Add chopped eggplant, egg, salt, garlic powder, ½ cup of flour, baking powder and chili powder or cayenne powder and continue chopping, or processing, until a thick puree is obtained.

❸ In a fry pan, add oil. When oil is hot, using a large wooden stirring spoon, drop mixture into hot oil. Fry until brown on both sides. Fry in batches until all of the mixture has been used.

❹ Drain well on paper towels. Serve hot.

Note:
While you are frying (step 3): you may need to add one or two more tablespoons of flour to the waiting celery-eggplant mixture to keep it thick because moisture is being released from the eggplant.

Try serving these tasty "latkes" or pancakes as a snack with a topping of yogurt, sour cream or applesauce. They also make an excellent vegetable to serve with any meal. They are more easily made in a food processor, but good results can be had by preparing by hand. In the latter case, it is important to chop the vegetables very fine.

Fast-Fried Eggplant

1 medium (12 ounce \ 340 gr)
eggplant, unpeeled, cut in
¼ inch (0.64 cm) round slices

olive oil

margarine

salt to taste

❶ **I**n a fry pan (preferably non-stick to minimize use of oil), start with 1 tablespoon each of olive oil and margarine.

❷ **F**ry eggplant slices in batches until soft and fairly dark brown on both sides. Add more oil and margarine as needed. Drain on paper towels.

❸ **A**dd salt and/or lemon juice to taste. Ready to serve.

Note:
Recipe can be doubled.

*W*hat could be simpler than this method of preparing eggplant? It needs only to be cut and fried to be enjoyed hot from the pan. I like it with salt; others add a squeeze of lemon juice. Serve it hot as a side vegetable. Or, when served warm or cold, it makes an ideal antipasto ingredient. It is difficult to estimate number of servings because in my family 2 slices per person is never enough.

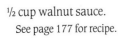

Fried Eggplant "Boats" With Walnut Sauce

½ cup walnut sauce.
See page 177 for recipe.

❶ **P**repare the walnut sauce. Reserve.

2 eggplants, 1 pound
(455 gr) each,
unpeeled

❷ **C**ut the eggplants in half lengthwise. Rub salt into the cut sides of the eggplants. Drain, cut side down, for 1 hour. Rinse and pat dry.

salt

4 cloves garlic, minced

❸ **I**n a small bowl, mix together the garlic, coriander and basil. Reserve.

1 tablespoon minced
fresh coriander
(cilantro)

1 tablespoon minced
fresh basil

❹ **A**dd ½ the olive oil to a skillet (preferably non-stick) large enough to accommodate all the eggplants, (or prepare in 2 batches). When olive oil is hot, add the eggplants, cut side down. Reduce heat to low, cover and cook for 8-10 minutes, or until cut sides are golden brown.

2-4 tablespoons olive
oil

❺ **T**urn the eggplants. Remove pan from heat. Cut a deep slash down the center of each eggplant. Do not cut through the skin. Stuff the garlic, coriander and basil mixture into the eggplant slices, reserving 1 teaspoon of the mixture.

❻ **R**eturn pan to heat. Add the remaining ½ of the oil to the skillet. Add 2-3 tablespoons of water. Cover and cook on low, skin side down, for 8-10 minutes, or until very soft.

❼ **R**emove to a serving platter. Spoon walnut sauce over the top of the filled eggplants. Sprinkle reserved garlic, coriander and basil mixture over the sauce. Serve hot or warm.

The walnut sauce makes these fried eggplant boats really special. The sauce is fast to make in the blender or food processor and can be prepared well ahead. And, once the eggplants have been salted and drained, they cook up quickly. Serve this eggplant dish as a main vegetarian meal with a large Nicoise salad or as a side vegetable with broiled meat, chicken or fish.

Grilled Eggplant

Parve
Serves 4

1 small (about 8 ounces \ 225 gr) eggplant

1 teaspoon vinegar

1 tablespoon vegetable oil

1 teaspoon Chinese sesame oil (optional)

1 teaspoon soy sauce

1 tablespoon pineapple juice

1 tablespoon white wine

❶ **W**ash eggplant. Cut away stalk and sepal. Cut eggplant in half lengthwise. Cut each half in thirds lengthwise. Then cut each third in half across. You should have 12 pieces.

❷ **P**lace eggplant pieces in a pot with water and cook until barely tender. Drain well. Place in a non-reactive (glass or ceramic) bowl.

❸ **I**n a small bowl, mix together all other ingredients. Pour mixture over eggplants and toss gently to coat eggplant. Place in refrigerator and allow to marinate for several hours. Turn occasionally.

❹ **G**rill in a wire grill basket in an oven or over hot coals. Turn and grill on other side.
Serve hot.

Micro Tip:
At Step 2, place eggplant pieces in a glass or ceramic bowl, cover and cook on High for 2-3 minutes, until eggplant is barely tender. Drain well. Then continue with Step 3.

In this recipe, the eggplant is very lightly cooked, then marinated in a flavorful Chinese-style marinade before grilling. It goes particularly well with other barbequed foods.

Hunan Style Eggplant

Parve
Serves 4 as a side vegetable
or as part of a Chinese meal

3 tablespoons oil

1 pound (455 gr) eggplant, peeled, cut in 1 inch (2.5 cm) chunks

2 cloves garlic, minced

1 teaspoon minced ginger root

2 teaspoons kosher hot bean sauce. See page 174 for recipe to make your own or see Note.

1 tablespoon soy sauce

2 teaspoons sugar

2 teaspoons parve chicken soup powder and ½ cup water

1 tablespoon vinegar

1 teaspoon oriental sesame oil

2 whole green onions, chopped

❶ **I**n a wok or skillet, heat 2 tablespoons of the oil. Add eggplant chunks, lower heat and stir-fry until soft, about 3 minutes. Remove from skillet. Reserve.

❷ **H**eat remaining tablespoon of oil in skillet. Add garlic, ginger root and bean sauce and stir-fry about 10 seconds.

❸ **A**dd soy sauce, sugar and stock. Bring to a boil.

❹ **A**dd vinegar and reserved eggplant. Mix well with the sauce. Cook additional minute.

❺ **S**tir in oriental sesame oil and green onions. Serve hot or at room room temperature.

Note:
Crumbled, dried chili peppers may be substituted for the hot bean sauce.

This quickly made stir-fry recipe comes from the south-west region of China where Szechwan and Hunan Provinces are noted for their fiery fare. Caution: the best way to enjoy its flavors and lingering aftertastes is to savor it slowly. If, at first taste, it is too fiery, the Chinese caution never to reach for a glass of water to put out the fire because that will make it worse. Instead, take a scoop of rice to douse the flame.

Chinese Stir-Fried Vegetables

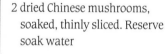

Parve
Serves 2 as a main meal;
4-6 as part of Chinese dinner

2 dried Chinese mushrooms, soaked, thinly sliced. Reserve soak water

1 teaspoon parve chicken soup powder

1 tablespoon soy sauce

2 teaspoons vinegar

½ teaspoon sugar

salt to taste

2 tablespoons vegetable oil

1 medium (10 ounces \ 285 gr) eggplant, unpeeled, cubed 1 inch (2.5 cm)

1 teaspoon minced garlic

1 teaspoon minced ginger root

½ medium onion, cut in thin, half moon slices

¼ cup thinly sliced carrot rounds

½ cup diced ½ inch (1.25 cm) green pepper

¼ cup julienned cucumber, unpeeled

1 cup diced tomatoes

2 tablespoons unsalted nuts

❶ **S**train the mushroom soak water. Combine ½ cup of the strained mushroom soak water with chicken soup powder, soy sauce, vinegar, sugar and salt. Reserve.

❷ **H**eat oil in a wok or deep fry pan. Add eggplant cubes and stir fry several minutes, until cubes begin to soften.

❸ **A**dd in the following order, stir frying for a minute after each addition: garlic, ginger root, onion, carrots, green pepper, cucumber.

❹ **P**ush vegetables to side of wok or pan. Add reserved mushroom soak water and spices. Bring to a boil until soup powder is dissolved. Stir to cover all vegetables in the wok or pan with this added liquid. Cover and cook several minutes. (Do not overcook. Vegetables should still be crisp.)

❺ **U**ncover and stir in reserved mushrooms and tomatoes until heated through. Remove to a serving dish and sprinkle nuts over top. Serve hot. Best served with rice.

As with most Chinese dishes, preparing the vegetables for stir-frying takes more time than the cooking. I find it convenient to cut up the vegetables (except the eggplant) early in the day and keep them covered in the refrigerator until ready to cook. Then, the last minute preparation and stir-frying is a "snap."

Creole Eggplant Casserole

Parve
Serves 4

For the Sauce:

½ tablespoon oil

1 heaping tablespoon chopped onion

1 heaping tablespoon diced green pepper

⅛ cup sliced mushrooms, fresh or canned

¼ cup diced celery

½ cup chopped fresh tomatoes

½ cup hot water

pinch salt

dash pepper

dash Tobasco sauce

⅛ teaspoon dried basil

⅛ teaspoon light brown sugar

For the Base:

1 small (6 ounces \ 170 gr) eggplant, cubed ½ inch (1.25 cm)

6 ounces (170 gr) zucchini, cubed ½ inch (1.25 cm)

For the Topping:

¼ cup bread crumbs

⅛ teaspoon dried oregano

⅛ teaspoon dried parsley

dash garlic powder

2 teaspoons margarine

❶ **T**o Make The Sauce: Add oil to a heated pot. Saute onion, green pepper, mushrooms, and celery for 5 minutes.

❷ **A**dd tomatoes, water, salt, pepper, Tobasco sauce, basil and brown sugar and simmer until thickened, about 30 minutes.

❸ **M**eanwhile, preheat oven to 350 F (180 C \ gas mark 4).

❹ **T**o Make The Base: Bring a pot of salted water to a boil. Add eggplant and zucchini cubes. Cover and boil about 10 minutes. Drain well.

❺ **G**rease an oven-proof casserole, or spray with non-stick spray. Layer part of the eggplant and zucchini cubes first, then part of the sauce. Continue layering, finishing with sauce.

❻ **T**o Make The Topping: In a small bowl, mix together bread crumbs, oregano, parsley and garlic powder.

❼ **S**prinkle bread crumb mix evenly over the top. Dot with margarine. Bake 30 minutes, until bubbling.
Serve hot.

---

*C*reole cookery is indigenous to Louisiana. The Acadians (Cajuns) combined classical French cuisine with Spanish and Anglo-Saxon cookery, blended with seasonings learned from the Choctaw and Chickasaw Indians and African Americans. This baked recipe makes a flavorful side-dish vegetable to serve with eggs, fish or meats.

Escalloped Eggplant

1 pound (455 gr) eggplant, peeled, cubed ½ inch (1.25 cm)

1 small onion, chopped

1 beaten egg

2 tablespoons plus 2 teaspoons melted margarine; reserve 2 teaspoons

¾ cup bread crumbs. Reserve ¼ cup

salt and pepper to taste

❶ **B**oil eggplant cubes in water 8-10 minutes until soft. Drain well.

❷ **I**n a bowl add eggplant cubes, onions, beaten egg, 2 tablespoons margarine, and ½ cup bread crumbs. Mix well.

❸ **P**our eggplant mixture in a greased ovenproof casserole, or one sprayed with non-stick spray. Cover with reserved ¼ cup bread crumbs and dot top with reserved 2 teaspoons margarine.

❹ **B**ake for 30 minutes in an oven 375 F (190 C \ gas mark 5). Spoon out to serve.
Serve hot.

*T*his is a good standby recipe that makes an excellent luncheon meal or a side vegetable for guests at dinnertime.

Potato & Eggplant Bake With Yogurt

1 pound (455 gr)
eggplant, unpeeled,
sliced lengthwise,
½ inch (1.25 cm)
thick

1 tablespoon lemon
juice

salt

2-3 large potatoes,
peeled, sliced
lengthwise, ½ inch
(1.25 cm) thick

1 tablespoon flour

1 tablespoon water

1 full cup yogurt

3 cloves garlic, minced

½ teaspoon dried dill

½ teaspoon salt

2-3 teaspoons olive oil

dash paprika

1 tablespoon snipped
parsley

❶ **A**dd eggplant slices, lemon juice and salt to a large bowl of cold water. Cover with a plate to keep the slices in the water. Keep in the water for 1 hour. Drain well.

❷ **A**dd potatoes to a bowl of cold water. Keep in the water for ½ hour. Drain.

❸ **B**oil potatoes 5 to 10 minutes, until slightly soft. Remove pan from flame and leave in the water another 2 to 3 minutes. Drain.

❹ **S**tabilize the yogurt: mix together the flour and water. Add to the yogurt. Add the garlic, dill and salt and mix well.

❺ **I**n a greased baking pan, or one sprayed with non-stick spray, lay potato slices to cover the bottom. Spread a drop or two of the olive oil and one teaspoon stabilized yogurt over each slice.

❻ **L**ay an eggplant slice over each potato. Spread a drop or two of the olive oil and 1 teaspoon stabilized yogurt over each slice. Continue layering potato and eggplant slices with olive oil and yogurt.

❼ **P**our remaining yogurt over the top. Sprinkle with paprika. Cover with aluminum foil. Bake at 350 F (180 C \ gas mark 4) for 45 minutes, or until potatoes are soft. Remove foil and bake another few minutes, until slightly browned on top. Sprinkle with parsley. Cut into squares.
Serve hot or cold.

This makes a nice side vegetable to serve with fish or eggs. It can also make a complete vegetarian meal accompanied by salads and vegetables.

Pumpkin & Eggplant Casserole

2 long eggplants, each about
   10-12 ounces (285-340 gr)

1 tablespoon salt

1 tablespoon lemon juice

3 tablespoons pine nuts

¾ pound (340 gr) pumpkin,
   peeled and cubed 1 inch (2.5 cm)

cooking oil for shallow frying.

1 very large or two medium
   onions, cut in half and sliced

4 cloves garlic, minced

2 tablespoons onion soup powder

pinch salt

pinch black pepper

6-7 tablespoons water

3-4 tablespoons finely grated
   kashkaval cheese

❶ Slice eggplants in half lengthwise. Slice each half lengthwise. Cut each piece across 1 inch (2.5 cm) thick. In a deep bowl, add eggplant pieces, water to cover, salt and lemon juice. Cover with a plate to keep eggplants immersed in the water. Leave for ½ hour, then drain eggplant pieces well. Dry with paper towels.

❷ In a fry pan, dry roast pine nuts, stirring until golden. Remove to small bowl. Reserve.

❸ Cook pumpkin covered in a little water until soft. Drain and reserve.

❹ Heat about ½ inch (1.25 cm) oil in a fry pan. Add eggplant (in two or three batches, adding more oil if necessary), and fry briefly on both sides until golden. Remove and drain well on paper towels.

❺ In the same fry pan, drain off all but one tablespoon oil. Add onions and garlic and fry until soft and golden. Add soup powder, salt, pepper and 3 tablespoons water.
Cover and cook 2-3 minutes.

❻ In a heatproof casserole, add eggplant, pumpkin, and onion mixture. Mix in. Add 3-4 tablespoons water. Sprinkle pine nuts and cheese over top.

❼ Cover casserole (with aluminum foil if casserole does not have a cover.) Bake at 350 F (180 C \ gas mark 4) for 25 minutes. Remove foil. Bake another 5 minutes.
Serve hot.

This makes a lovely side vegetable dish served with broiled fish. It is also good with an all vegetable meal. I've even served it as a simple luncheon meal, with a side tomato, cucumber, radish salad dressed only with vinegar. It is a rich dish and is best served with simple foods.

Mexican Stew

2 very large onions, thinly sliced

2 tablespoons margarine

2 tablespoons vegetable oil

1 pound (455 gr) eggplant,
unpeeled, cubed ½ inch
(1.25 cm)

6 canned, drained, peeled whole
tomatoes, cut up

1 teaspoon salt

½ teaspoon hot chili pepper
(cayenne powder)

⅓ cup prepared salsa

2 cups frozen or canned, drained
corn kernels

½ cup sliced black pitted olives

❶ **I**n a large wok or pan, lightly saute the onion in
the margarine and oil.

❷ **A**dd the tomatoes, eggplant, salt, hot chili pepper
and prepared salsa. Cover. Cook on low heat for
20-25 minutes, until eggplant is softened.

❸ **A**dd the frozen or canned corn and sliced olives.
Cover. Cook another 10 minutes until heated
through.
Serve hot.

This easily prepared vegetable stew brings the flavor of colorful Mexico to life. Enjoy it over rice or other grain. For the adventurous, try serving it as a topping for spaghetti. A side salad rounds out the meal.

Meatless Lions Head

1 pound (455 gr) eggplant

1 teaspoon salt

3 tablespoons finely minced
scallion, white and green, firmly
packed

2 tablespoons finely minced
parsley leaves

2 tablespoons finely minced celery

½ teaspoon finely grated fresh
ginger

dash black pepper

⅓ cup chickpea flour

½ teaspoon mushroom soup
powder

½ teaspoon parve chicken soup
powder

½ teaspoon soy sauce

vegetable oil for deep frying

18 chinese cabbage leaves,
washed, cut in 2 inch (5 cm)
pieces

For the Stock

1 tablespoon parve chicken soup powder

1 cup water plus 2 tablespoons water

1 tablespoon soy sauce

1 tablespoon cornstarch

Note:
*Best to use smaller eggplants as they tend to
have less seeds.*

Lion's Head is a delicious Chinese stew. The dish gets its name because the meatballs and cabbage suggest the mane of a lion. We have substituted eggplant for the meat that is used in the usual recipe. You won't miss it.

cont. ▷

Parve
Serves 2 as a main meal;
serves 4 as part of a Chinese meal

❶ **P**eel and coarsely grate eggplant. Mix in salt. Allow to drain ½ hour. Squeeze out as much water as you can.

❷ **T**ransfer squeezed, dry eggplant to a bowl. Add minced vegetables, grated ginger, black pepper, chickpea flour, mushroom soup powder, ½ teaspoon chicken soup powder and ½ teaspoon soy sauce. Mix well. Form 12 walnut size balls.

❸ **I**n a wok or other deep pan, fry "meatballs" until very dark brown. Fry in batches, if necessary, turning so the "meatballs" are brown all over. (It should look like beef.) Remove with a slotted spoon. Drain well on paper towels. Reserve.

❹ **R**emove all but 1 tablespoon oil from the pan. Heat oil. Add cabbage leaves and stir-fry until slightly softened, about 2 minutes. Transfer to an earthenware or heavy pot, lining the bottom and sides with the cabbage leaves.

❺ **I**n a separate small pan, heat stock: the 1 tablespoon parve chicken soup powder, 1 cup water and the 1 tablespoon soy sauce. Pour over cabbage leaves. Simmer, covered, until cabbage leaves are soft, about 20 minutes.

❻ **P**lace fried "meatballs" on cabbage leaves. Bring stock to a boil. Cover. Cook 10 minutes more. Transfer only the cabbage leaves to a serving bowl, with "meatballs" on top, leaving the stock in the pot.

❼ **I**n a small bowl, blend cornstarch and remaining 2 tablespoons water. Bring the stock back to the boil. Add the blended cornstarch and water to the boiling stock remaining in pan. Cook, stirring until stock thickens. Pour sauce over "meatballs".
Serve hot with rice.

Microwave Eggplant Casserole

Parve
Serves 4-6 as a side dish
Serves 9 on a buffet

margarine

2 pounds (905 gr) eggplant, peeled, sliced

1 teaspoon salt

1 clove garlic, crushed

1 egg, slightly beaten

2 tablespoons margarine, melted

1 medium onion, chopped

½ cup dry breadcrumbs or matzo meal

1 teaspoon dried basil

½ teaspoon pepper

1 teaspoon lemon juice

1 tablespoon sesame seeds

paprika

❶ **G**rease an 8×8 inch (20.3×20.3 cm) microwave-safe dish with margarine. Do not use non-stick spray.

❷ **I**n a very large microwave-safe bowl, bring 1 inch (2.5 cm) of water to a boil. Add eggplant slices, salt and garlic. Cover with plastic and microwave on high 5 to 8 minutes until eggplant slices are very soft.

❸ **I**n a small microwave safe dish, melt 2 tablespoons margarine in microwave for 30 seconds to 1 minute.

❹ **D**rain eggplant slices. Discard garlic. Press out moisture. Transfer to bowl or food processor. Reduce eggplant slices to a pulp, with a fork or in the food processor.

❺ **A**dd egg, melted margarine, onion, breadcrumbs or matzo meal, basil, pepper, lemon juice and sesame seeds and blend in well.

❻ **S**pread eggplant mixture evenly in the greased dish. Dust surface with paprika. Microwave uncovered on high for 10 to 14 minutes, until firm. Let cool before cutting into serving pieces. Serve warm or at room temperature.

This casserole is quickly made in the microwave. The sesame seeds add protein and a bit of crunch to the smooth texture of this vegetable dish. It makes an excellent side vegetable with any meal.

Ratatouille

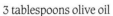

3 tablespoons olive oil

2 medium onions, thinly sliced in half moons, separated

1 large green pepper, thinly sliced lengthwise.

½ medium sweet red pepper, thinly sliced lengthwise.
See Note.

½ medium sweet yellow pepper, thinly sliced lengthwise

1¼ pounds (570 gr) eggplant, unpeeled, cubed ½ inch (1.25 cm)

½ pound (225 gr) zucchini, cut in thinly sliced rounds

3 medium tomatoes, diced

1 teaspoon dried parsley

½ teaspoon dried oregano

½ teaspoon dried basil

1 teaspoon minced garlic

2 tablespoons lemon juice

1 teaspoon brown sugar

salt to taste

❶ **H**eat oil in a large pot. Add onions and saute until transparent.

❷ **A**dd green, red, and yellow peppers and eggplant cubes. Saute, stirring continuously about 5 minutes. Do not allow bottom to burn.

❸ **S**tir in zucchini and tomatoes. Cover pan and simmer under low heat for 30 minutes, stirring occasionally. (Do not add water; the vegetables will simmer in their own released juices.)

❹ **S**tir in parsley, oregano, basil, garlic, brown sugar, salt and lemon juice. Cook uncovered 10-15 minutes more until vegetables are well mixed, appear stew-like and some of the liquid has evaporated.
Serve hot or cold.

Note:
If sweet red and/or yellow peppers are unavailable, use additional green peppers.

This classic French vegetable dish can be served as a side vegetable, a salad or even a main meal. Proportions are not very important so feel free to add or substract any ingredient to your taste. For added flexibility, this recipe can also be made in the microwave.

Steamed Eggplant

Parve
Serves 4

2 cups water

1 medium (12 ounces \ 340 gr)
 eggplant

dash salt

dash garlic powder

2 teaspoons lemon juice

1 teaspoon olive oil

dried dill

❶ **B**ring water to a boil in a wok or steamer. Place a rack in the wok or steamer.

❷ **L**eave eggplant with stalk and sepal. Wash. Place eggplant in heat-proof dish or pan.

❸ **P**lace dish or pan on the rack. Cover and steam for 10 minutes, or until eggplant is easily pierced with a fork. Remove.

❹ **W**hen cool enough to handle, remove stalk. Cut eggplant lengthwise in four equal pieces. On the pulp side, slash each piece in three places.

❺ **O**n each piece of eggplant, in the following order, add: salt, and garlic powder; drizzle ½ teaspoon lemon juice and ¼ teaspoon olive oil over each surface; sprinkle dill over top.
Serve hot or cold.

One of the simplest and quickest ways to prepare eggplant is to steam it. It goes well with any meat dish, but has a particular affinity for lamb. The recipe is intended to serve each person one-quarter eggplant, but it can be easily doubled to serve eight.

Stuffed Potatoes

*Dairy
Serves 4*

4 large potatoes

4 pieces sun dried
tomatoes

1 teaspoon balsamic
vinegar

1 tablespoon olive oil

1 small onion,
chopped

1 clove garlic, minced

½ pound (225 gr.)
eggplant, peeled, cut
in ¼ inch (0.64 cm)
dice

¾ teaspoon salt

dash black pepper

½ cup yogurt

⅛ cup minced parsley

❶ **W**ash, pierce, and bake potatoes. While potatoes are baking, prepare the filling.

❷ **W**ash dried tomatoes. Place in a small pot. Cover with boiling water. Add balsamic vinegar. Simmer until tomatoes are very soft, about 5 to 10 minutes. Strain in a small-holed strainer, reserving vinegar water. Rinse tomatoes and drain thoroughly. Chop or cut tomatoes into small pieces.

❸ **I**n a heated earthenware pot, add olive oil. When oil is hot, add onions and garlic. Fry for 2-3 minutes. Add chopped tomatoes. Fry 2 minutes.

❹ **A**dd diced eggplant. Stir until eggplants are well coated with onions, garlic and tomatoes. Add salt and pepper.

❺ **A**dd 3 tablespoons of reserved strained balsamic vinegar water. Cover. Lower heat. Cook 10-15 minutes until eggplant is very soft. Add more reserved balsamic vinegar water if necessary to prevent eggplant from sticking to pot.

❻ **W**ith the back of a wooden spoon, or fork, coarsely mash eggplant mixture. Remove from stove. Cool slightly. Add yogurt and parsley.

❼ **T**o serve: Make one deep slash, or a cross-cut in each baked potato. Do not cut all the way through. Squeeze potato gently to open. Spoon one-quarter of filling into each potato. Serve. Extra filling may be served in a small dish on the side.

These stuffed potatoes make an excellent dairy lunch or dinner. Serve with a large tossed salad and pickles for lunch. For dinner, add another cooked vegetable to round out the meal. Try the filling alone as a salad or cold side vegetable.

Swiss Chard & Eggplant Pancakes ("Latkes")

Parve
Makes about 12

1 medium (12 ounces \ 340 gr) eggplant, peeled, cut in large cubes

1 tablespoon vinegar

2 large stalks Swiss chard, finely chopped

1 small onion, chopped

¼ cup chopped parsley

1-2 cloves garlic, minced

2 teaspoons lemon juice

1 egg

6 tablespoons flour (or more as needed)

½ teaspoon baking powder

½ teaspoon salt

dash pepper

pinch red hot pepper (cayenne pepper)

vegetable oil for frying

❶ Cook eggplant cubes and vinegar in boiling water to cover until eggplant is very tender. Drain well.

❷ Add eggplant cubes and all other ingredients, except vegetable oil, to a food processor and puree.

❸ In a fry pan, add oil. When oil is hot, using a large wooden stirring spoon, drop mixture into hot oil. Fry until brown on both sides. Fry in batches until all of the mixture is used.

❹ Drain well on paper towels. Serve hot.

Micro Tip:
At Step 1, cook eggplant cubes and vinegar in a moderate amount of water on High for 5 to 7 minutes. Proceed to Step 2.

These unusual pancakes or "latkes" make a satisfying side vegetable to any meat or dairy meal. Instructions call for the use of a food processor which makes preparation fast and easy.

Tri-Color Peppers & Eggplant

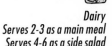

Dairy
Serves 2-3 as a main meal
Serves 4-6 as a side salad

1 pound (455 gr) eggplant,
 unpeeled

1½ teaspoons salt

vegetable oil for shallow frying

1 medium green pepper

1 medium red pepper

1 medium yellow pepper

1 cup yogurt

2-3 cloves garlic, minced

salt to taste

❶ **C**ut eggplant lengthwise in ¼ inch (0.64 cm) thick slices. Then cut each slice 3 inches (7.5 cm) long.

❷ **S**alt the eggplant and allow to drain for 20 minutes. Pat dry, pressing the eggplant slightly to squeeze out any moisture.

❸ **H**eat some oil in a large fry pan (preferably non-stick). Fry eggplant slices until softened and golden on both sides. Fry in batches, adding more oil as needed. Drain well on paper towels. Reserve. Allow to cool.

❹ **C**ut peppers lengthwise in ½ inch (1.25 cm) thick slices. In the same fry pan, lightly brown peppers, about 3-5 minutes, stirring constantly. Remove from pan. Allow to cool.

❺ **I**n a medium bowl, mix together the yogurt, garlic and salt to taste.

❻ **T**o serve: Place fried eggplant slices on a large serving platter. Toss fried peppers over the eggplant slices. Spoon yogurt and garlic mixture over all.
Serve cool.

*T*his makes an ideal light warm weather vegetarian supper. Serve it surrounded with salads or steamed vegetables, such as broccoli. It can easily double as a side salad with fish or other vegetarian meals.

Tiny Stuffed Eggplants

4 tiny (3 to 4 inches long \ 7.5 to 10 cm) eggplants

1 tablespoon kosher salt

1 tablespoon sesame seeds

1 tablespoon unsweetened desiccated (dry) coconut

¼ teaspoon ground hot red pepper (cayenne powder)

1 tablespoon coriander seeds

1 teaspoon ground cumin

2 tablespoons vegetable oil

1 medium onion, chopped

3 cloves garlic, minced

⅛ teaspoon turmeric

2 teaspoons sugar

1 tablespoon lemon juice

1 cup water

❶ **W**ash eggplants well, keeping the stalks and sepals. Cut each eggplant lengthwise in 4 places, coming within ½ inch (1.25 cm) of stalk and sepal. (Do not cut all the way though). Rub about ⅛ teaspoon of kosher salt into each cut section. Stand upright in a colander and drain 45 minutes to 1 hour.

❷ **M**eanwhile, prepare the spices. Heat a skillet and dry roast together the sesame seeds, coconut, hot red pepper, coriander and cumin for 2 to 3 minutes, stirring continuously. Remove spices. Cool. Grind spices in a blender or mortar and pestle. Set aside.

❸ **G**ently squeeze out excess moisture from eggplants. Wipe dry. Set aside.

❹ **P**repare the stuffing: Heat oil in a skillet large enough to hold eggplants in one layer. Add onion and garlic. Fry until golden. Remove skillet from heat. Add ground spices, turmeric, sugar, and 1 teaspoon of the kosher salt to the onion and garlic.

❺ **R**eturn to the fire with a low heat. Mix ingredients and cook, stirring for 1 minute. Add lemon juice and ½ cup water, cooking until sugar dissolves. Remove mixture to a bowl.

❻ **S**poon about a teaspoonful or more of stuffing into each cut section of reserved eggplants. Lay stuffed eggplants in one layer in the same skillet. (Place any extra stuffing in the skillet.)

❼ **A**dd another ½ cup water. Bring to a boil, lower heat and simmer covered, until eggplants are very tender, about 30 to 45 minutes, depending on size of eggplants. While eggplants are cooking, turn several times with tongs by the stalk, spooning sauce over eggplants each time. (Add a little more water if necessary.)

❽ **T**o Serve: Remove eggplants to a platter. With a slotted spoon, remove any excess stuffing. Spoon stuffing and some of the sauce over eggplants.
Serve hot.

Tiny eggplants are a seasonal speciality, so buy them when you can, to make this moderately spicy Indian recipe. This tiny stuffed eggplant is unusual because the filling must be inserted into lengthwise cuts in the whole eggplant. Serve as a side vegetable or as an appetizer.

Vegetable Curry

Dairy
Serves 4 as a main meal
Serves 6-8 as a side vegetable

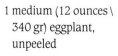

1 medium (12 ounces \ 340 gr) eggplant, unpeeled

2 medium-large (total 12 ounces \ 340 gr) potatoes, peeled

1 cup frozen okra

1 cup frozen whole green beans

1 cup frozen baby carrots

2 tablespoons olive oil

1 tablespoon butter or margarine

3 cloves garlic, minced

1 teaspoon garam masala. See Note B.

1 teaspoon turmeric

large pinch hot red pepper, to taste (cayenne pepper)

1½ cups yogurt

¼ teaspoon salt

½ teaspoon dried mint, rubbed

dash paprika

2 teaspoons snipped parsley (optional)

❶ **C**ut eggplant crosswise in ¼ inch (0.64 cm) thick slices. Cut any large slices in half. Salt and allow to drain for 30 minutes. Rinse, pat dry.

❷ **C**ut potatoes crosswise in ¼ inch (0.64 cm) thick slices. Boil until just softened, about 15 minutes. Drain.

❸ **S**et out frozen vegetables to defrost slightly. If any of the baby carrots are too large and thick, cut in half lengthwise.

❹ **I**n a wok or large pot, add olive oil and butter or margarine and fry eggplant slices very briefly. Add more oil if needed.

❺ **M**ix in potatoes, okra, green beans and carrots.

❻ **I**n a small bowl, mix together 1 minced garlic clove, garam masala, turmeric and hot red pepper. Add to vegetables and mix well. Cover and cook on low heat 30 to 45 minutes, until eggplant slices are tender and potatoes are soft. Stir vegetables frequently. If stew becomes too dry, and begins to stick and brown on the bottom, then add 1 to 2 tablespoons hot water.

❼ **M**eanwhile, prepare yogurt sauce: In a medium bowl, mix yogurt, 2 garlic cloves, salt and mint.

❽ **R**emove vegetables to a serving dish. Spread garlic yogurt sauce over all. Sprinkle with paprika and parsley. Serve warm.

Notes:

A: This is a dry curry where the use of frozen vegetables serves to provide the water to steam the vegetables. If you prefer to use fresh vegetables, clean the fresh okra, green beans and carrots; parboil and drain before adding to the potatoes in Step 5.
Then, at Step 6, you may need to add an extra 1 or 2 tablespoons of water to provide enough moisture to steam the vegetables.
B: Garam masala is a mixture of various spices extensively used in Indian cooking. It can be bought in Indian markets. If unavailable, mix your own. See page 174 for recipe.

Vegetable Medley

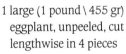

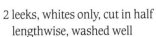

1 large (1 pound \ 455 gr) eggplant, unpeeled, cut lengthwise in 4 pieces

2 leeks, whites only, cut in half lengthwise, washed well

2 tablespoons olive oil

1½ cups chopped tomatoes

2-3 fresh sage leaves, chopped or ¼ teaspoon dried sage

3 tablespoons coarsely chopped fresh basil leaves

¼ cup white wine

1 teaspoon brown sugar

salt and pepper to taste

❶ **B**roil eggplant pieces and leeks, cut side up, until lightly browned.

❷ **C**ut the broiled eggplant pieces into ½ inch (1.25 cm) cubes. Slice leeks across 1 inch (2.5 cm).

❸ **I**n a fry pan (preferably non-stick), heat 1 tablespoon oil. Saute leeks until softened. Remove from pan. Reserve.

❹ **A**dd remaining 1 tablespoon oil to pan. Add eggplant cubes. Saute, stirring over medium-high heat about 5 minutes until softened.

❺ **S**tir in reserved leeks, tomatoes, sage and basil. Add wine, brown sugar, salt and pepper. Cook another 5 minutes.
Serve warm or hot.

Leeks are used extensively in Welsh cooking, and are in fact the national emblem of Wales. As the story goes, in the sixth century a victorious Welsh army attached leeks to their helmets to distinguish their troops from the enemy. This recipe, however, owes its flavors more to Provence, the southeastern section of France on the Mediterranean, than to Wales. Serve it as a side vegetable.

Beans Grains & Pasta

Brown Rice Pilav

1 tablespoon plus 2 teaspoons
  butter or oil

3 tablespoons desiccated (dry)
  shredded or flaked coconut

1 cup uncooked brown rice
  (preferably long grain)

1 medium (about 12 ounce \
  340 gr) eggplant, peeled, cubed
  ¼ inch (0.64 cm)

½ cup yogurt

salt to taste

pepper to taste

cumin to taste

❶ **M**elt 1 teaspoon butter or oil in a fry pan
(preferably non-stick). Add coconut and fry,
stirring until golden. Remove to a small bowl.
Reserve.

❷ **M**elt 2 teaspoons butter or oil in a pan. Add rice
and fry, stirring until kernels are coated and some
of them begin to turn white. Add 2 cups water.
Cover closely. Bring to a boil, then lower heat and
simmer about 30 minutes or until kernels are soft.
Remove from pan and cool.

❸ **M**elt 2 teaspoons butter or oil in a pot or fry pan
(preferably non-stick). Add eggplant cubes. Fry,
stirring occasionally, until eggplant is almost
tender. Cover and cook over low heat several more
minutes until eggplant is soft. Remove from pan
and cool.

❹ **W**hen rice and eggplant are cooled, mix them
together in a serving bowl. Mix in reserved
coconut and yogurt, salt, pepper and cumin
to taste.

Note:

*Serve at room temperature or cold. When dish is to be
served cold, taste and adjust seasonings.*

*T*his dish is based on a Turkish recipe. The brown rice gives it a pleasant nutty flavor. When
at room temperature, it can be served as a side vegetable. When cold, it can be served as a
salad.

Buddhist Mock Chicken

Parve
Serves 2 as a main meal
Serves 4-6 as part of an oriental meal

2 dried Chinese mushrooms, soaked in hot water until soft, sliced thinly. Strain soaking water and save

1 tablespoon kosher hoisin sauce

1 tablespoon kosher hot black bean sauce. See Note.

1 tablespoon soy sauce

1 tablespoon parve chicken soup powder plus 1 cup hot water

6 ounces (170 gr) frozen tofu, defrosted, squeezed dry of moisture

6 ounces (170 gr) eggplant, unpeeled

2 tablespoons oil

1 teaspoon ginger root, minced

3 cloves garlic, minced

1 medium sweet green pepper, cut in 1 inch (2.5 cm) squares

1 medium onion, sliced

❶ **I**n a bowl, mix reserved mushroom water, hoisin sauce, hot black bean sauce, soy sauce and parve chicken soup powder and water. Reserve.

❷ **S**lice tofu in ¼ inch (0.64 cm) slices across widest part of the block, then cut each slice in half, making squares approximately 1½×2 inches (3.75×5 cm). Reserve slices.

❸ **S**lice eggplant ¼ inch (0.64 cm) lengthwise. Then cut into 1½ inch (3.75 cm) squares. (These should be about the same size as the tofu.) Salt and leave for 15 minutes. Then rinse and drain very dry.

❹ **H**eat oil in a wok or large pan. Add ginger root and garlic. Fry briefly. Add in the following order, stir-frying after each addition: eggplant, green peppers, onions, and mushrooms. Add reserved mushroom water mixture to wok or pan. Bring to a boil. Lower heat.

❺ **A**dd reserved tofu slices. Spoon sauce over tofu slices until the slices have absorbed the sauce. Cover and cook until vegetables are softened but still crisp.
Serve hot over fried noodles or with rice.

Note:

If store bought kosher hot bean sauce is unavailable, make your own. See page 175 for recipe. Alternatively, use crumbled dried red chili peppers for the desired spicy flavor.

Buddhists are vegetarians, but they have clever ways of utilizing vegetables to look and taste like meat. In this recipe the role of chicken is played by tofu, a soybean product which is available in health food stores and many supermarkets. The recipe may look complex, but it is as simple as most oriental stir-fry dishes.

Eggplant & Rice Quiche

Dairy
Serves 4 as a meal
Serves 8 as an appetizer

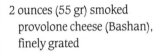

3 eggs

2 ounces (55 gr) smoked provolone cheese (Bashan), finely grated

1½ cups cooked long grain white rice

1 medium (10 ounces \ 285 gr) eggplant, peeled, cubed ½ inch (1.25 cm)

1 whole green onion, minced

¼ cup canned sliced mushrooms, drained

salt and pepper to taste

pinch paprika

For the Shell:

❶ Lightly grease a pie pan (9 inches \ 22.8 cm) or spray with non-stick spray.

❷ Beat 1 egg and combine it with 1 ounce grated cheese and all the cooked rice. Press the mixture into the bottom of the pie pan and up the sides. Set aside.

For the Filling:

❶ Bring ½ cup water to a boil. Add eggplant cubes. Cook covered until soft. Drain well.

❷ In a medium bowl, beat 2 eggs. Mix in the eggplant, onion, remaining cheese, mushrooms, salt, pepper and paprika. Pour mixture into the rice shell.

❸ Bake in 375 degree F (190 C \ gas mark 5) oven about 40 minutes, until quiche is set and brown. Let stand a few minutes before cutting into wedges.
Ready to serve.

A quiche is a hot cheese pie which is thought to have originated in the Alsace-Lorraine region of France. There are many variations. Some quiches add mushrooms; others add fish; and some use eggplant as we do here. This rich-flavored quiche will be welcome at lunch or at a light supper, accompanied by a crisp tossed lettuce salad. It finds favor, too, as an appetizer or at a buffet table.

Vegetable Bean Loaf

2 cups mashed
  roasted eggplant
  from 1½ pounds
  (680-700 gr)
  eggplants. See page
  172 for Basic Roast
  Eggplant recipe.

1 heaping cup cooked
  or canned chick peas
  (garbanzo beans),
  drained. See Note.

½ cup sunflower seeds

½ cup snipped fresh
  celery leaves

½ cup warm water

1 teaspoon sugar

1 tablespoon yeast

1½ cups matzo meal

1 cup finely minced
  green onion, whites
  and greens

2 eggs, beaten

1 teaspoon salt

pinch black pepper

1 teaspoon dried
  zaytar or dried
  oregano

1 teaspoon poppy
  seeds

❶ **P**repare eggplant as indicated. Reserve.

❷ **C**oarsely chop chick peas. (This is best done in a
  food processor).

❸ **I**n a dry fry pan, preferably non-stick, lightly toast
  sunflower seeds over moderate heat, stirring continuously.
  Remove seeds from pan and reserve.

❹ **I**n the same pan, toast celery leaves until they are dry and
  crisp, stirring continuously. (They will reduce down to about
  ⅛ cup.) Reserve.

❺ **I**n a small bowl, add water and sugar. Dissolve sugar.
  Sprinkle yeast over the top and allow to froth.

❻ **I**n a large bowl, add matzo meal, mashed roasted eggplant,
  chopped chick peas, sunflower seeds, celery leaves, and
  green onion, mixing thoroughly after each addition.
  (A mixer with a dough hook is useful).

❼ **M**ake a well in the center, add beaten eggs, salt, pepper and
  zaytar or oregano and mix again thoroughly.

❽ **G**rease a 2 pound loaf pan, or spray with non-stick spray.
  Spoon the eggplant mixture into the pan, patting down
  evenly. Sprinkle poppy seeds over the top.

❾ **A**llow to rise in a warm place about 30 minutes until the
  loaf rises just above the rim. Bake in a preheated oven
  350 F (180 C \ gas mark 4) 35-40 minutes, or until a wooden
  toothpick comes out clean. Allow to cool before slicing.
  Keeps well, wrapped in foil in refrigerator.

Note:

*See page 173 for recipe on how to cook chick peas
(garbanzo beans).*

This unusual loaf is equally at home with meat or dairy meals, as a side vegetable or as a
vegetarian meal. It can also serve as a bread and makes a nice "nosh" when topped with a thin
slice of cheese. Try a slice for breakfast for a high protein start to the day.

Channa Baigan Tarkari

4 large leaves Swiss chard
(mangold)

1 teaspoon minced ginger root

pinch dried diced red chili pepper
(cayenne)

¼ teaspoon black mustard seeds

¼ teaspoon fennel seeds

½ teaspoon cumin seeds

pinch asafetida powder (hing)
(optional). See Note A.

pinch chili powder (cayenne)

pinch black pepper

¼ teaspoon dried ground
coriander (cilantro)

¼ teaspoon paprika

1 tablespoon vegetable oil

2 cups canned chopped tomatoes
with juice

½ cup boiling water

1 medium (10-12 ounces \
285-340 gr) eggplant

1 can chickpeas (garbanzo beans),
drained

salt to taste

dash Tobasco sauce

1 teaspoon garam masala.
See Note B.

❶ **W**ash well, and coarsely chop Swiss chard leaves
and stalk. Allow any water that clings to the
leaves to remain. Reserve.

❷ **I**n a small dish, place minced ginger root, dried
diced red chili pepper, black mustard seeds, fennel
seeds and cumin seeds. Reserve.

❸ **I**n another small dish, place asafetida, chili
powder, black pepper, dried ground coriander, and
paprika. Reserve.

❹ **H**eat vegetable oil in a 3 quart (3 liter)
earthenware pot. When oil is hot, add all the
spices from the first small dish that contains the
minced ginger root. Fry, stirring, until seeds
begins to brown.

❺ **A**dd spices from the second small dish, fry
1-2 seconds only. Immediately add tomatoes.
Bring to a boil over medium heat. Cook
10 minutes, stirring occasionally until sauce
is reduced and separating.

cont. ▷

❻ While tomatoes are cooking, wash and cut eggplant into ½ inch (1 cm) cubes.

❼ Add boiling water to tomatoes. Bring back to the boil. Add eggplant cubes, chick peas and reserved chopped Swiss chard, stirring after each addition of vegetables and beans. Add salt to taste. Cover and simmer 25 minutes.

❽ Add Tobasco sauce and garam masala. Continue cooking for 5 minutes more.
Serve hot.

Notes:
A: Asafetida powder (hing) is available at Indian markets. In Indian cookery, hing is often used to reduce the flatulence caused by eating beans.
B: Garam masala is an Indian spice mixture available in Indian and specialty markets. To make your own, see instructions on page 174.

This flavorful eggplant and chickpea stew is based on a traditional Indian recipe. All its spices are available in local super markets or Indian stores. As it contains no meat, it makes an excellent vegetarian meal, served either with or without rice as an accompaniment. Stuff any leftovers into a pita for a quick snack or lunch on-the-go.

Japanese-Style Noodles

Parve
Serves 2. Doubles easily

1 tablespoon pine nuts

3½ ounces (100 gr) soba noodles

½ teaspoon vegetable oil

½ tablespoon (7.5 ml) olive oil

1½ cups eggplant, cubed ½ inch (1.25 cm)

1 cup broccoli florets

2 tablespoons soy sauce

1 tablespoon water

dash black pepper

dash garlic powder

¼ teaspoon oriental sesame oil

❶ **A**dd pine nuts to a heated dry non-stick fry pan. Toast lightly, stirring constantly. Remove from pan. Reserve.

❷ **P**ut up a large pot of water to boil. Add soba noodles and vegetable oil to boiling water. When slightly softened, stir to separate noodles. Cook until al dente, about 5-7 minutes. Drain. Rinse in cold water. Drain again. Keep warm.

❸ **W**hile noodles are cooking, add olive oil to non-stick fry pan. Add eggplant and fry, stirring continuously for 2 minutes.

❹ **A**dd broccoli florets and fry 1 minute. Add soy sauce, water, black pepper, and garlic powder. Cover. Lower heat and continue cooking until eggplant is soft, about 5 minutes.

❺ **D**ivide noodles into separate bowls. Drizzle half the oriental sesame oil over each bowl of noodles. Toss lightly to cover. Add half the eggplant and broccoli mixture to each bowl of noodles. Top each bowl with half the reserved pine nuts. Ready to serve.

You might find this dish featured on the menu of oriental noodle-bars, a new type of fast-food eatery which has become popular in the west. When you are looking for something different, and perhaps a little exotic, this recipe fits the bill. It uses soba, a buckwheat noodle that is wheat-free. Soba can be found in oriental, Indian and health food stores.

Rice & Eggplant Pilav

Parve
Serves 4

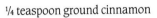

¼ teaspoon ground cinnamon

¼ teaspoon ground cumin

¼ teaspoon hot red pepper
  (cayenne pepper)

¼ teaspoon black pepper

¼ teaspoon turmeric

¼ teaspoon ground cloves

½ teaspoon salt (optional)

4 tablespoons plus 1 teaspoon
  vegetable oil

3 tablespoons flaked desiccated
  (dry) coconut

1 cup dry long grain rice, cooked a
  day ahead, refrigerated

1 large (1 pound \ 455 gr)
  eggplant, unpeeled, cubed ¼ to
  ½ inch (0.64 to 1.25 cm)

1 medium onion, chopped

¼ cup finely snipped, well packed
  fresh coriander (cilantro)

❶ **M**ix cinnamon, cumin, cayenne pepper, black pepper, turmeric, cloves and salt in a small bowl. Reserve.

❷ **H**eat 1 teaspoon oil in a fry pan (preferably non-stick). Add coconut and fry, stirring, until golden. Remove to a small bowl. Reserve.

❸ **H**eat 2 tablespoons oil in the same fry pan. Add reserved mixed spices, stirring about 2 minutes. Remove pan from heat.

❹ **W**hile the pan is off the heat, add eggplant to the spices and toss until well coated. Add onions and toss again. Return to a low to medium flame and cook, stirring, until eggplant is soft, about 15 minutes. Cover and continue to cook 5 to 10 minutes more until eggplant is very tender.

❺ **H**eat 2 tablespoons oil in a large saucepan or wok. Add cooked rice and fry, stirring and breaking up any lumps until the rice is heated through. Mix the eggplant in the rice and heat for several minutes. Mix in coriander leaves.

❻ **T**o serve: arrange eggplant and rice mixture on a large platter. Sprinkle the reserved fried coconut over the top. Serve immediately. Or, may be kept unrefrigerated for several hours in a tightly closed container.
Reheat to serve.

This pilav makes a lovely presentation with the purple skin of the eggplant and the bright green of the coriander contrasting with the stark white of the rice. The use of coconut marks its origins in India, but this dish is also popular in North Africa. It goes well with any meal.

Mexican Stuffed Eggplant

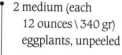

2 medium (each
12 ounces \ 340 gr)
eggplants, unpeeled

2 cups cooked kidney
beans or 1 can
kidney beans,
drained. See Note.

2 tablespoons water

1 tablespoon parve
beef soup powder

2 teaspoons chili
sauce, or ketchup

2-3 cloves garlic,
minced

salt and pepper to taste

1½ tablespoons olive
oil

2 ounces (55 gr)
cheddar cheese,
grated

❶ **W**ash trimmed eggplants. Cut in half lengthwise. From the sepal end, (the widest part), measure 3 inches (7.5 cm) of pulp. Hollow out only this area, leaving a shell ¼ inch (0.64 cm) thick. (This is a "half boat.") Reserve the pulp. Salt the eggplants. Turn upside down to drain.

❷ **F**inely chop the reserved pulp. In a food processor, add chopped pulp, kidney beans, water, parve beef soup powder, chili sauce or ketchup, garlic, salt and pepper. Process until beans are well mashed and become thickened. (Without a food processor, mash kidney beans and add ingredients as indicated above, combining and mashing until thickened.) Reserve mixture.

❸ **R**inse eggplant half-boats in cold water. Pat dry. Place them upside down on a heat proof dish. Steam 10-15 minutes or until soft.

❹ **M**eanwhile, in a non-stick fry pan, or heavy skillet, heat 1 tablespoon olive oil. Add bean mixture. Cook uncovered on medium heat for 10 minutes, until any moisture has evaporated and mixture becomes very thick. Stir continuously.

❺ **H**eat oven to 350 F (180 C \ gas mark 4). Grease a baking tray with non-stick spray or oil. Place eggplants on baking tray and fill each shell with ¼ of the bean mixture. With the remaining ½ tablespoon olive oil, drizzle a little over the unstuffed portion of the eggplants.

❻ **B**ake for 15-20 minutes. Remove from oven. Sprinkle grated cheese all over eggplants. Return to oven and bake a few more minutes until cheese melts. Serve hot.

Note:

To cook beans: sort and wash 1 cup of dry beans. Soak overnight in 3 cups of water, ½ teaspoon salt. Drain. Add beans to a large pot with 3 cups of fresh water, ½ teaspoon salt and 1 teaspoon oil. Simmer beans two hours, or until tender.

This version of stuffed eggplant uses a flavorful kidney bean mixture, but other types of beans can be used as well. Try navy beans, pinto beans, black beans or cranberry beans.

Lasagna

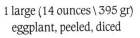

1 large (14 ounces \ 395 gr) eggplant, peeled, diced

2 tablespoons olive oil

⅛ teaspoon minced garlic

1 medium onion, chopped

2 medium tomatoes, chopped

½ teaspoon dried oregano

½ teaspoonn dried basil

½ teaspoon parve beef soup powder

dash black pepper

2-3 tablespoons chopped fresh coriander (cilantro) or parsley

2 egg whites, beaten

1 cup dry cottage cheese or ricotta

6 ounces (170 gr) mozzerella cheese, coarsely grated, about 1½ cups, reserve ½ cup

⅓ cup finely grated Parmesan cheese

6 lasagna noodles, cooked

❶ **S**alt diced eggplant. Allow to drain ½ hour. Rinse, drain and dry in a kitchen towel.

❷ **I**n a fry pan, heat the olive oil. Add garlic and onions and saute until soft. Add diced eggplant and saute 3-4 minutes. Add tomatoes, oregano, basil, beef soup powder, black pepper and coriander. Cook until tomatoes are wilted. Remove mixture to a large bowl. Cool slightly.

❸ **A**dd beaten egg whites, dry cottage cheese or ricotta, 1 cup mozzerella cheese and Parmesan cheese. Mix well.

❹ **P**reheat oven to 350 F (180 C \ gas mark 4). Grease (or use non-stick spray) a lasagne pan (11¼ × 7½ × 1¾ inches \ 30 × 19 × 4.5 cm).

❺ **L**ayer 3 noodles in the pan, overlapping slightly. Spread ½ of the vegetable-cheese mixture evenly over noodles. Repeat with the remaining noodles and vegetable-cheese mixture. Sprinkle reserved ½ cup mozzerella cheese over top.

❻ **B**ake ½ hour. Remove from oven. Allow to stand for 10 minutes. Cut into serving pieces.

You can enjoy this light-tasting vegetarian-cheese lasagna even if you are dieting or watching your cholesterol count because the fat content has been pared down by using low fat cheeses and only the whites of eggs.

Savory Quick Bread

3 cups self-rising flour

½ cup wheat germ

1 teaspoon salt

1 teaspoon sugar

3 large cloves garlic, minced

1 medium onion, coarsely grated

½ cup finely grated mozzarella cheese

1 teaspoon finely chopped sun-dried tomatoes

1 heaping cup unpeeled, coarsely grated eggplant

1 teaspoon dried basil, rubbed

1 cup milk

½ cup water

paprika

❶ In a large bowl, mix flour, wheat germ, salt, sugar, minced garlic, grated onion, grated cheese, chopped tomatoes, grated eggplant and dried basil.

❷ Stir in milk and water. Mix well into a thick, very sticky batter.

❸ Turn into a well oiled loaf pan, approximately 10×5×2½ inches (25.4×13.7×6.5 cm). Level top with slightly dampened fingers. Dust top with paprika.

❹ Bake in the oven on the middle shelf at 350 degrees F (180 degrees C \ gas mark 4) for 1 hour. Turn out. Cool on a wire rack. Serve cut in ½ inch (1.25 cm) slices.

This is a fairly dense savory bread which takes only a few minutes from mixing bowl to oven. Both in appearance and taste it is intriguing: flecked with unpeeled eggplant and dried tomatoes and laced with garlic, onions and cheese. Serve it with vegetarian or fish meals.

Tempeh Stuffed Eggplant

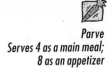

Parve
Serves 4 as a main meal;
8 as an appetizer

2 medium-large (14-16 ounces \
395-455 gr) eggplants, unpeeled

1 package (8 ounces \ 225 gr)
tempeh, defrosted

3 tablespoons olive oil

¼ cup sliced green olives

½ cup tomato paste

½ cup hot water

½ cup spicy, chunky salsa

½ cup canned chopped tomatoes
with juice

salt and pepper to taste

---

❶ **W**ash trimmed eggplant. Cut in half lengthwise. Scoop out pulp, leaving a shell ¼ inch (0.64 cm). (I find the use of a grapefruit spoon helpful). Salt the shells. Turn upside down to drain. Reserve the pulp.

❷ **S**team defrosted tempeh 10 minutes. (This helps to open the pores.) When cool enough to handle, coarsely grate the tempeh.

❸ **L**ightly salt and chop the reserved eggplant pulp. Fry pulp in 2 tablespoons hot olive oil for 3 minutes. Lower heat. Cover. Cook another 3 minutes. (Pulp will have reduced to half).

❹ **A**dd remaining 1 tablespoon olive oil to pulp. Add grated tempeh. Fry, adding sliced olives after 1 minute. Fry briefly again. Stir in tomato paste, hot water, salsa, tomatoes and salt and pepper to taste.

❺ **R**inse shells. Dry with paper towels. Stuff eggplant shells with equal amounts of tempeh mixture.

Note:
To serve as an appetizer, cut each eggplant shell in half crosswise.

❻ **I**n a large baking pan, add hot water to ½ inch (1.25 cm). Place eggplants in baking pan, filling side up. Bake uncovered at 350 F (180 C \ gas mark 4) 45-50 minutes until shells are soft. Serve hot.

This moist eggplant dish is a good introduction to the use of tempeh, a soy bean product invented in Indonesia. Today tempeh is sold frozen in health food stores. It is popular with vegetarians because of its high protein content. As with all bean products, it is best served with a grain, cheese or yogurt to provide all the required amino acids found in meat. (Topped with cheese or yogurt makes this a dairy dish).

Tofu & Eggplant In A Skillet

Dairy
Serves 4-5

1 medium onion, chopped

4 cloves garlic, minced

½ cup sliced canned mushrooms, drained

2 tablespoons olive oil

1 small can (3½ ounces \ 100 gr) tomato paste

¾ cup hot water

2 teaspoons parve chicken soup powder

¼ teaspoon dried oregano

¼ teaspoon dried basil

¼ teaspoon garlic powder

salt to taste

1 pound (455 gr) eggplant, peeled, cubed ¼ inch (0.64 cm)

1 pound (455 gr) frozen tofu, defrosted, drained, squeezed dry and crumbled

3 eggs, lightly beaten

1 cup coarsely grated cheddar cheese

❶ In an oven-proof skillet, fry onion, garlic and mushrooms in olive oil for 5 minutes.

❷ In a bowl, mix together tomato paste, water, parve chicken soup powder, oregano, basil, garlic powder and salt.

❸ Add eggplant cubes and tomato paste mixture to skillet. Bring to a boil, reduce heat, cover and simmer for 15 minutes, until eggplant has softened.

❹ In a separate bowl, mix together the crumbled tofu, beaten eggs and cheddar cheese. Stir into eggplant-tomato mixture.

❺ Bake in the skillet in a 350 F (180 C \ gas mark 4) oven for 35 minutes. Allow to set for several minutes. Cut into wedges and serve.

Tofu, derived from soy beans, is an ancient Japanese and Chinese food. It is finding more and more acceptance on Western tables for its high quality, meatless protein. This recipe makes an easy one-dish family meal. It needs only a light salad to complement the rich protein of tofu, eggs and cheese.

Desserts & Sweets

Candied Eggplant

5 tiny (about 3 to 4 inches \ 7.5 to 10 cm) eggplants

8½ ounces (240 gr) powdered sugar

¾ cup water

1-2 pieces of stick cinnamon

¼ cup lemon juice

Note:
For variety, instead of a burnt sugar syrup, stop cooking after Step 4. Remove eggplants. Discard cinnamon stick.

❶ **W**ash eggplants well with skin, stalk and sepal. Pierce 2 or 3 times with a fork.

❷ **I**n a pot large enough to hold all the eggplants, add the eggplants. Add cold water to cover. Bring water to boil. Cover. Cook 10 minutes, occasionally pushing down the eggplants into the water. Remove eggplants, drain and cool.

❸ **I**n the same pot, add the powdered sugar and ¾ cup water. Bring to a boil. Boil furiously, stirring until sugar is dissolved. Lower flame and cook 5 minutes more, to make a thin syrup. Add cinnamon and lemon juice.

❹ **G**ently squeeze out excess water from eggplants. Add to syrup. Bring syrup to a simmer. Cook uncovered about 30 minutes on a medium flame. With tongs, turn eggplants at the stalk from time to time.

❺ **A**fter 30 minutes, allow syrup to come to a rolling boil. Continue cooking until syrup turns brown, turning eggplants occasionally. Remove eggplants. Discard cinnamon stick.

❻ **S**erve whole, warm or cold. Allow the diner to discard the stalk. Eat all the skin and pulp.

This is one of the most unusual desserts you are ever likely to serve. It is best made with very small eggplants, either the purple or white ones. Save any extra syrup for topping grapefruit or apple slices.

Candied Eggplant Skins

Parve
Makes about 1¹/₄ cups

½ cup sunflower seeds

5½ ounces (140 gr) washed eggplant skins

⅓ cup water

1 cup sugar

1 tablespoon lemon juice

¼ teaspoon ground ginger

⅛ teaspoon cinnamon

❶ **D**ry roast sunflower seeds in a fry pan, stirring until slightly brown. Remove to a bowl. Reserve.

❷ **C**ut eggplant skins into thin pieces about 1½ inches (3.75 cm) long.

❸ **A**dd water to a pot. Add sugar. Cook until sugar dissolves and becomes syrupy.

❹ **A**dd eggplant skins, lemon juice, ginger, cinnamon and sunflower seeds. Cook until the eggplant skins look almost translucent and the syrup has turned a pinkish-purple. (Any eggplant pulp that may have remained on the skins will cook away).

❺ **R**emove to a clean glass jar with a tight lid. When cool, place in the refrigerator.

This is a sweet treat which can be used in many ways to enhance everyday desserts. Try it mixed with stewed fruit, and in fruited gelatin. And the piece de resistance: as a topping for ice cream. (This recipe requires a large number of eggplant skins which can be accumulated by saving the skins from other recipes. Put them aside in a plastic bag or container in the refrigerator.)

Chocolate Eggplant Drop Cookies

Parve
Makes about
80 cookies

¾ cup eggplant (about 6-7 ounces \ 170-200 gr), peeled, cubed ½ inch (1.25 cm)

2 cups sifted flour

⅛ cup unsweetened cocoa

1 teaspoon baking powder

1 teaspoon baking soda

1 teaspoon cinnamon

½ teaspoon salt

½ cup shortening or margarine

1 scant cup sugar

1 tablespoon vanilla sugar

1 egg

1 teaspoon vanilla

❶ **P**reheat oven to 350 F (180 C \ gas mark 4).

❷ **C**ook eggplant cubes in ½ cup boiling water until very soft. Drain well. Puree in food processor or mash well by hand. Reserve.

❸ **I**n a large bowl, combine flour, unsweetened cocoa, baking powder, baking soda, cinnamon and salt.

❹ **I**n a medium bowl, cream together shortening and sugars.

❺ **B**lend in egg and vanilla to creamed mixture. Add to flour until well mixed.

❻ **A**dd eggplant and beat until combined.

❼ **O**n a greased cookie sheet, drop dough from a teaspoon 1½ inches (3.75 cm) apart. Bake 10-12 minutes. Remove from cookie sheet. Store in a closed container.

These yummy, moist chocolate cookies taste, for all the world, like pumpkin. If they are not gobbled up immediately after baking, they freeze well.

Coconut, Raisin & Eggplant Muffins

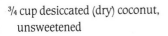

Ingredients:

¾ cup desiccated (dry) coconut, unsweetened

2 cups self-rising flour

2 teaspoons salt

½ cup sugar

¾ cup finely grated peeled eggplant

⅓ cup raisins

1 egg, beaten

¼ cup oil

½ cup milk

½ cup pineapple juice

Instructions:

❶ In a non-stick fry pan, lightly toast ½ cup desiccated coconut. Reserve ¼ cup untoasted.

❷ In a large bowl stir together flour, salt, sugar, ½ cup toasted desiccated coconut, grated peeled eggplant and raisins, stirring after each addition. Make a well in the center of the flour mixture.

❸ In a medium bowl, whisk together the beaten egg, oil, milk and pineapple juice.

❹ Pour all at once into the well in the center of the flour mixture. Stir lightly and quickly together. The batter should be lumpy. Spoon into oiled muffin tins, two-thirds full.

❺ Sprinkle tops with reserved untoasted desiccated coconut. Bake in a pre-heated oven 400 degrees F (200 C \ gas mark 6) for 20-22 minutes.

This is a sweet muffin, good as a mid-morning snack or dessert.

Eggplant Marmalade

Parve
Yields 3 to 4 pints

IMPORTANT: Jams and marmalades made with gelatin and a low acid vegetable such as eggplant should be frozen or stored in the refrigerator for safety.

3 pounds (1.35 kilos) eggplant

6 cups sugar

½ cup bottled lemon juice

1 cup crushed, drained canned pineapple

2 packages (3 ounces \ 85 gr) kosher apricot flavored gelatin

❶ **C**oarsely grate 6 cups of peeled eggplant. By handfuls, squeeze out the liquid.

❷ **I**n a large pot, cook grated eggplant slowly, until soft and tender, about 10-15 minutes, stirring to prevent sticking. Separate the grated pieces with a wooden spoon while cooking and stirring.

❸ **A**dd sugar and lemon juice. Stir over low heat to dissolve sugar.

❹ **A**dd crushed pineapple. Bring mixture to a rolling boil. Cook about 6 minutes.

❺ **R**emove from the heat and slowly add gelatin, stirring with each addition. Continue stirring until gelatin is dissolved, at least 2 to 3 minutes.

❻ **P**our into hot sterilized jars, allowing ½ inch (1.25 cm) head room. Cover.

❼ **W**hen cool, put the amount you intend to use immediately in the refrigerator. Store the excess in freezer.

Many vegetables are made into jams, marmalades and preserves and eggplant is no exception. It is a refreshing change from ordinary jams and has a delightful flavor. Of course, it can be served the more traditional way on toast, pancakes and waffles, but it is also excellent used as a basting sauce (perhaps mixed with a little BBQ sauce or ketchup) for roasting chicken or beef. When stored in attractive small jars, it makes a welcome gift.

No-Oil Muffins

6 ounces (170 gr) eggplant, peeled, diced

water

1¾ cups white flour

2½ teaspoons baking powder

¾ teaspoon salt

¼ cup sugar

1 egg, beaten

½ cup freshly squeezed orange juice, with pulp

¼ cup milk

¼ cup chopped walnuts

❶ **C**ook peeled, diced eggplant in a small amount of boiling water until soft, about 3-5 minutes. Drain very well, squeezing out as much water as you can, coarsely mashing eggplant in the process. Reserve.

❷ **I**n a large bowl, sift together white flour, baking powder, salt and sugar. Make a well in the center.

❸ **I**n a smaller bowl, combine beaten egg, orange juice, milk, reserved eggplant and walnuts.

❹ **A**dd all at once to the dry flour ingredients. Stir just until moistened.

❺ **F**ill well-greased muffin pans ⅔ full. Bake at 400 degrees F (200 degrees C \ gas mark 6) for 20-25 minutes, until lightly browned on top.

These tasty muffins are made without oil for the calorie-conscious among us.

Mock Pumpkin Mousse

2 pounds (905 gr) eggplant, peeled, cubed 1 inch (2.5 cm)

1 egg

¼ cup white sugar

¼ cup brown sugar

1 tablespoon cornstarch (cornflour)

2 packages unflavored kosher gelatin

¼ cup cold orange juice

1 cup boiling water

½ teaspoon ground ginger

½ teaspoon ground cinnamon

½ teaspoon nutmeg

1 teaspoon grated orange rind

½ cup heavy cream, whipped

❶ **C**ook eggplant cubes in boiling water until very soft. Drain very well. For a smooth mousse, discard excess eggplant seeds which separate from the flesh. (It is impossible to remove them all.) Puree in a food processor or mash by hand. (Should yield 2 heaping cups pureed.) Remove, cool and reserve.

❷ **I**n a food processor, blend together egg, white sugar, brown sugar and cornstarch.

❸ **I**n a small bowl, combine gelatin and orange juice and add it to the egg, sugar and cornstarch mixture. Process briefly. Add boiling water and process until blended.

❹ **A**dd reserved pureed eggplant, ginger, cinnamon, nutmeg and orange rind. Process until well blended. Remove mixture to a bowl.

❺ **F**old whipped cream into eggplant mixture. Chill until set.

❻ **T**o serve, return chilled, set mixture to food processor. Puree until you have a light, mousse-like texture. Spoon into serving cups. If desired, top mousse with a dollop of yogurt or whipped cream.

Note:
Cover and refrigerate any extra servings.

This tasty dessert has a real pumpkin flavor. It is best made in a food processor. For true mousse texture, it should be processed again after chilling, as indicated below. However, if put immediately into serving dishes, and chilled until set, it also can be served as a pudding.

Eggplant Preserves

Parve
Makes about 5 cups

1 cup fresh grapefruit juice, strained. See Note A.

3 tablespoons lemon juice

2 pounds (905 gr) sugar

2 pounds (905 gr) eggplants, unpeeled

1 apple, grated with peel. See Note A.

Notes:

A: Save the pits from the grapefruit. Save the pits and cores from the apple. (They contain pectin, needed to help gel the syrup). Stuff pits and cores into a metal tea caddy, or wrap tightly in a mesh or cloth bag.

B: To test for the setting stage: Place a tablespoon of syrup on a clean plate. Place in refrigerator for 3 to 5 minutes. If it firms up and forms a "skin", it is ready. If not, continue cooking.

---

❶ **I**n a large pot, add grapefuit juice, lemon juice and sugar. Bring to a boil. Lower heat to a simmer and cook until a syrup is formed.

❷ **M**eanwhile, wash and trim eggplants of stalks and sepals. Cut in half crosswise. Cut each half lengthwise in "fingers" ¼ inch (0.64 cm) thick julienne strips. Discard excess seed pockets.

❸ **A**dd the julienned eggplant, grated apple and enclosed pits and cores to the pot. Bring to a boil and continue cooking until eggplant strips are clear and syrup has reached the setting stage. (This may take 1 to 1½ hours. See Note B for testing the setting stage). Remove the enclosed pits and cores.

❹ **P**our preserves into a clean, large baking pan and stir fruit pieces evenly throughout the syrup. Allow to cool. Then add to sterilized jars, allowing ½ inch (1.25 cm) head room. Cover and freeze or refrigerate.

---

*T*his versatile sweet has many uses. Try it over ice cream or mixed with yogurt and perhaps some meuseli for breakfast or dessert. Add it to stir-fry dishes instead of sugar. For its use in a refreshing drink, see page 168 for our Tamarind Beverage recipe. And, when packed in attractive jars, these preserves make welcome gifts.

This eggplant recipe is called a preserve because the fruit is in large pieces and retains its shape, is clear and shiny, plump and tender. The syrup is clear and varies from the thickness of honey to that of soft jelly. IMPORTANT: As with any low acid vegetable, it should be stored in the refrigerator or frozen for safety.

Tamarind Beverage

Parve
Makes 6-10 glasses

1 cup water

½ cup packed Eggplant Preserves.
See page 167 for recipe.

¼ cup packed prepared tamarind
pulp. See Note B.

❶ **T**o make the syrup: in a blender, add water and eggplant preserves. Blend well until the preserves become pulp. Add tamarind concentrate and blend again briefly until a thickened, but pourable syrup is made.

❷ **T**o make one drink: in a tall glass, combine ⅛ to ¼ cup syrup (to taste) with 1 cup very cold water or soda water. Stir well. Add an ice cube if desired.

Notes:

A: Store unused syrup in a closed container in the refrigerator.

B: The prepared (processed) tamarind concentrate sold in Indian markets and health food stores is not kosher. To prepare a kosher version, see page 176 for recipe.

The tamarind tree of India produces a fruit which has a natural sour seasoning which is used like lemon. It makes a refreshingly cool summertime drink. Folklore maintains that the drink is especially good for digestion and is helpful in treating seasickness. In my version, the addition of eggplant preserves adds sweetness and texture that is lacking in the usual method of preparation.

Nutty Tea Loaf

Parve
Makes 1 loaf

3 eggs

¾ cup oil

¾ cup sugar

1 teaspoon vanilla

1 pound (455 gr) eggplant

1½ cups self-rising flour

1 teaspoon ground cinnamon

1 teaspoon ground allspice

¾ cup chopped pecans or walnuts

❶ **P**reheat oven to 350 F (180 C \ gas mark 4). Grease a 2 pound loaf pan (or use non-stick spray). Lightly flour the base. Set aside.

❷ **I**n a large bowl, beat together eggs, oil, sugar and vanilla until light.

❸ **P**eel and coarsely grate eggplant. Squeeze very dry. You should have 1 cup closely packed eggplant. Stir into egg mixture.

❹ **B**lend together flour, cinnamon and allspice. Add to egg and eggplant mixture. Stir in chopped nuts until well blended.

❺ **P**our into reserved greased, floured loaf pan. Bake in the middle of the oven for 1 hour to 1 hour and 10 minutes. Test with a toothpick to be sure it is baked through. Cool in the pan for 5 minutes. Then turn out on a wire rack. Cool completely before slicing.

In numerous taste tests, no one has ever guessed that this quick-to-prepare dessert contains eggplant. Serve it at a mid-morning or afternoon coffee break or top it with ice cream.

Miscellaneous Recipes

Basic Roast Eggplant

1 whole unpeeled eggplant with the stalk and sepal kept on. Note that more than one eggplant may be roasted at a time, using any of the methods indicated below.

❶ **W**ash the eggplant in the customary way you wash your fruits and vegetables.

❷ **T**he eggplant may be roasted in one of three ways:
A: Over an open flame on a stove top or BBQ grill
B: Under an open flame in a gas oven grill
C: In a hot oven (400 F \ 200 C \ gas mark 6), pierced twice with a sharp knife

These three methods differ in the time it takes to roast the eggplant and in its flavor. A 1 pound eggplant takes about 45 minutes to bake in an oven (C). It roasts much quicker under or over an open flame (A and B), in perhaps 20 minutes, but must be watched more closely and turned more often.

❸ **I**f A or B above is used: Using tongs, carefully turn the eggplant by the stalk until the skin is dark and blistered all over. When cool enough to handle, remove stalk and peel skin carefully, removing as much of the skin and burnt particles as you can. Run peeled eggplant under cold water to remove clinging burnt particles. (It is impossible to remove them all.) Drain well.

Note:

By the addition of the lemon juice, salt and pepper in Step 5, the roasted chopped or mashed eggplant prepared in this way can be served as a simple salad.

If C above is used: Using tongs, carefully turn the eggplant by the stalk until the skin is soft when tested with a finger and wrinkled all over. Turn several times while baking. When cool enough to handle, remove stalk and peel eggplant. Drain well.

❹ **A**s specified in the particular recipe you are preparing, either chop or mash eggplant by hand or puree in food processor.

❺ **I**f preparing ahead, add 1 tablespoon lemon juice, salt and pepper to the chopped or mashed eggplant. Mix gently. Remove to a glass or non-reactive bowl. Cover and refrigerate until ready to use.

*R*oasting eggplant imparts a special smokey flavor. It is the basic step in the preparation of many eggplant salads and cooked foods. Above are three different ways to roast eggplant. Check the recipe you intend to prepare to determine if a particular roasting method is suggested. Note too whether the directions tell to chop or mash the eggplant in Step 4 above.

How To Cook Chick Peas
(Garbanzo Beans)

Parve
Makes about 2 cups

1 cup chick peas (garbanzo beans)

6 cups water

1 teaspoon salt

2 teaspoons vegetable oil

A. Long soak method:

❶ **S**ort and wash 1 cup dry chick peas.

❷ **S**oak 6-8 hours or overnite in 3 cups water and salt. Drain.

❸ **T**o a large pot, add soaked, drained chick peas with 3 cups fresh water and oil.

❹ **B**ring to a boil. Lower heat. Cover. Simmer 2 hours, or until chick peas are tender but still firm. (Chick peas never get really soft.)

B. Quick soak method:

❶ **S**ort and wash 1 cup dry chick peas.

❷ **P**lace in a large pot with 3 cups of water, salt and oil. Bring to a boil. Cook 2 minutes. Remove pot from heat. Let stand 1 hour.

❸ **R**eturn to heat. Bring water back to a boil. Lower heat and simmer chick peas about 1½ hours or more, until tender. (Chick peas never get really soft.)

Listed above are two ways to cook chick peas. The first method requires a long soaking before cooking; the second is a quick-soak method. I prefer the long soak method because I believe it produces a larger bean, but the quick-soak method is fine when time is limited. Either method also can be used to cook other types of beans, such as kidney beans, navy beans, cranberry beans, etc.

Garam Masala

Parve
Makes 2¹/₂-3 tablespoons

1 tablespoon cardamon seeds

1 teaspoon whole cloves

1 teaspoon black peppercorns

1 teaspoon ground cumin

1 teaspoon ground cinnamon

❶ **I**n a blender or coffee grinder, add cardamon seeds, cloves and peppercorns. Grind until powdery.

❷ **A**dd cumin and cinnamon and blend.

❸ **S**tore in a jar with a tight lid. Lasts indefinitely.

Garam masala is a mixture of various spices used extensively in Indian cookery. It can be bought ready-made in Indian markets, or it is just as easy to mix your own with this recipe.

Hot Black Bean Sauce

Parve
Makes about ⅓ cup

3 tablespoons salad oil

1½ tablespoons ground hot chili pepper (cayenne pepper)

1½ tablespoons salted black beans, rinsed and drained. See Note.

1 tablespoon minced garlic

2 teaspoons dry sherry or white wine

1 teaspoon oriental sesame oil. See Note.

¼ teaspoon salt (optional)

❶ In a glass jar or heat proof bowl, mix together all ingredients. Cover tightly with aluminum foil. Steam on a rack over simmering water for half an hour. Cool. Refrigerate covered. Lasts indefinitely.

Micro tip:

In a micro safe bowl, mix together all ingredients. (Use a large enough container for the bean sauce mixture so that it does not boil over during cooking). Cover with plastic. Fill another micro-proof container with 1 cup of water. Microwave both on Medium for 7-10 minutes. Discard water. Cool bean mixture. Refrigerate covered.

Note:

Salted black beans and oriental sesame oil are available in oriental markets.

Hot black bean sauce is also known as hot bean paste. This is a fairly spicy sauce that is used sparingly in Chinese stir-fry dishes and it is also used as a dipping sauce. The non-kosher sauce is sold in oriental markets or you can make your own kosher version following this recipe.

Tamarind Pulp

1 tamarind brick

2 cups very hot water

❶ **B**reak off ½ pound (225 gr) tamarind from the brick. Tear into small pieces.

❷ **I**n a pot, bring the hot water and tamarind pieces to a boil. Lower heat and simmer for at least 10 minutes.

❸ **T**ransfer the softened tamarind and liquid into a sieve placed over non-interactive bowl.

❹ **W**ith your fingers, or the back of a wooden spoon, push through the sieve as much pulp as you can.

❺ **T**o extract more pulp, transfer the remaining tamarind in the sieve into a bowl with ½ cup very hot water. Mash. Return to the sieve and extract more pulp, scraping the bottom of the sieve to collect all the thick strained pulp. Discard the seeds and woody fibers. It is now ready to use.

To store:

Keep unused portion in a container in the refrigerator. Keeps in the refrigerator for 2 weeks. Freezes well. Keep remaining portion of the brick for another use.

---

*T*amarind is the vitamin-rich fruit of the tamarind tree. It is used extensively in Indian cookery as a souring agent, much as we use lemon. It is sold in two forms in Indian markets. One form is processed tamarind concentrate which contains only the pulp and is ready to use. This form is not kosher.
The second type of tamarind sold comes in its unprocessed natural state, retaining the seeds and woody fibers of the fruit. From this form you can make your own kosher tamarind pulp. This type comes wrapped in cellophane in one pound (455 gr) bricks. When buying the brick, choose one that is slightly pliable to make it easier to use.

Walnut Sauce

¾ cup walnuts

1 tablespoon walnut oil

½ tablespoon white wine

½ tablespoon vinegar

¼ cup coarsely chopped onions

1 clove garlic, minced

2 teaspoons parve chicken soup
  powder and ¾ cup water

½ teaspoon dried dill or
  1 tablespoon minced fresh dill

1 teaspoon minced fresh coriander
  (cilantro)

salt and pepper to taste

❶ **I**n a blender or food processor, add the walnuts and process until a fine crumble. Add the oil and process until well blended.

❷ **A**dd all other ingredients and process until well blended. Remove to a bowl. Reserve.

To store:

Keep covered in refrigerator. Will keep several days. To serve, warm it briefly and pour over food or serve as a separate sauce.

---

*T*his sauce is fast to make in the blender or food processor and can be prepared several days in advance. It is good served with fish, chicken and over lightly cooked vegetables such as broccoli and cauliflower.

Berbere

⅛ cup chopped onions

2 cloves garlic, minced

2 tablespoons oil

¼ cup red chili powder (cayenne)

1 teaspoon minced fresh ginger

¼ teaspoon ground cardamon

¼ teaspoon ground cloves

¼ teaspon allspice

¼ teaspoon ground nutmeg

¼ teaspoon cinnamon

1 tablespoon flour

½ cup water

❶ In a small pan, saute onion and garlic in hot oil until soft. With a fork, mash them in the pan.

❷ Add the chili powder, all the spices and flour. Saute over low heat until thoroughly mixed. (You may need to add a little more oil.)

❸ Slowly add the water, stirring constantly over very low heat. Raise the heat to medium. Bring to a boil, stirring until a thickened paste is formed. (The paste will get much thicker as it cools.) It is now ready to use.

To store:
Transfer the thickened paste to a small glass jar or container. Pack it tightly. When cool, add enough oil over the top to cover ¼ inch (0.64 cm). Cover. Refrigerate. It can be kept refrigerated for up to 6 months by replenishing the oil on top after each use.

Pronounced "barbaray", berbere is an exotic, fiery hot paste used extensively in Ethiopian cookery. Similar spice mixtures are used in Latin America, Southeast Asia, Africa and the Middle East. It can be used wherever you want to add a fiery taste to your food.

Coconut Milk

1¼ cups desiccated (dry) coconut (unsweetened)

1¼ cups boiling water

❶ **P**lace coconut and water in a food processor or blender and blend for 3-5 minutes.

❷ **P**our into a jar and allow to cool for ½ hour.

❸ **S**hake well. Strain through 3-4 thicknesses of cheesecloth, or other loosely woven fabric, squeezing out as much milk as possible.

❹ **D**iscard the remaining coconut. The milk is ready to use or store in a covered glass container in the refrigerator.

Note:

When the milk is stored, the coconut cream (the richer part) will rise to the top. The cream can be spooned out and used in recipes that call for coconut cream, or stirred back into the milk and used as coconut milk.

Coconut milk is an important ingredient in Thai and Indonesian cooking. The canned coconut milk which we buy in oriental and health food stores is made from fresh coconut and is quite rich. If it is not available in your area, you can make an acceptable substitute following the recipe above which uses dried coconut. For a richer milk, use 2 cups of coconut to the same amount of water.